Finding Your Prince

Paige Nicole Weslaski

Copyright © 2015 Paige Weslaski

All rights reserved.

ISBN-10:1515341755
ISBN-13: 978-1515341758

Follow Paige at
www.milknhoneyministries.com

Paige Nicole Weslaski

James, Mom, Dad

Julia Ismail, Amy Cummins, Carolin Wuttke, Gina Martin, Hanna Wilbershide, Hanna Sokol, Britt Kidd, Savannah Janssen, Dana Iverson, Alisa Danzer, Amy Papillon, Brianna Chu, Cassie Papaioannou, Bethany Boeck, Mary Jo Krum, Stephanie Bailey, Krystal Carr, Andrea Kacynski, Mal Dygert, Joanne Kourtknee, Becca Shrenker, Hannah Tuinstra, Blaire Williams, Kara Smoot, Katie Parker, Aubrey Stenson, Julie Contreras, Jordan Chambliss, Brian Gonzales, Chad Arents, and 'Ignite' Class 7.

Dr. John Jones, Dr. Gary Selby, Dr. Stone Watt, Dr. de los Santos, Dr. Stoltzfus, Dr. Willis, Pastor Brian and Nancy La Spada, Susan Giboney, Miss Ruth Jensen, Janet Moore, Amy Deburgh, Miss Mayra, Janet Evert, Lena Giffoni, Linda Truschke, Thomas Fitzpatrick, Mrs. Dean, Mrs. Malacara, Pastor Tim Chaddick.

Dedicated to Grandma Shirley, the world's classiest grandmother.

Paige Nicole Weslaski

Introduction

"Just because you don't have a prince doesn't mean you're not a princess."
- Zayn Malik, former member of One Direction

Peering through the mango trees, he found her. She was the most gorgeous woman he'd ever seen, standing just a few feet away. Right before his eyes, there she was: picking sunflowers and giggling in one of the most beautiful valleys in the garden. Adam, God's first creation, finally found the match he'd been waiting for. With a twinkle in her eye and no ring on her finger, she was everything he could want in a woman.

She instantly became his prized possession. He loved the way she styled her dark hair, the way she bathed in the moonlight, and the way her big brown eyes shone in the sun. After courting her, it became official: they were husband and wife.

He couldn't have been happier with her. She climbed the highest trees to collect their favorite fruit, making her specialty dish of banana mashed potatoes. He combed her coarse, black hair and held her rough hands, leathered from working hard in the garden.

After weeks of marriage, God asked Adam to name all the animals. Adam named the camel, the walrus, the chipmunk, the dove, and the pink fairy armadillo, searching far and wide to find those that scurried and those that flew and those that galloped.

After a long day of work, he eased his body onto a vine-stitched hammock, and his wife tossed him a freshly picked banana as he closed his eyes for a nap.

"Adam!" he heard from behind.

Popping up, he quickly called back, "Yes, my Lord?"

"Why are you relaxing when your job isn't finished? I thought I told you to name every animal in the garden?"

"Um, God, I did. I searched everywhere and named each one! I did all you asked! Didn't you hear me calling out their names? Didn't you see me looking under rocks, hiking massive mountains, and checking deep caves? There's no way I could've missed even one!"

Shaking His head back and forth, God slowly lifted His finger to the being in the hammock next to Adam: his wife, his beloved, his cherished.

Disgusted, Adam fired back: "No! What, what are you trying to say God? You're calling my wife an animal?! How dare you! She's my precious gem, how could you say such a thing?!"

With a look of compassion, God softly put his hand on Adam's shoulder. "Adam. My dear, sweet Adam. That is not your wife. She's... a gorilla! How could you not see the differences? Did you think because she was the most similar to you than the others she was your match? My dearest son, if you'd only waited a few more days, I would have presented you a real woman, one you'd relate to on every level! A strong, confident, loving daughter of mine, not an animal. I've been preparing her in Heaven for months and had even given her a beautiful name: Eve. What were you thinking?"

Astonished, confused, and embarrased, Adam hung his head in despair and asked the gorilla for his diamond back. Why hadn't he just waited for the perfect girl? Why did he try to convince himself the gorilla was his true love? Didn't he see the blatant differences between them, like how she could eat dozens and dozens of bananas every day or how her dark hair covered her entire body? He'd wondered why she was so good at climbing trees. It was all starting to make sense. No wonder she peeled bananas with her feet, she was a gorilla for goodness sakes! Why didn't he just ask God for a companion?

Like this fictional version of Adam, our culture tells us we need to find a mate as soon as possible in order to achieve ultimate acceptance, security, and fulfillment.

As single gals, it's tempting to think like our culture thinks. But thankfully, God has a better plan: we don't have to fall for the wrong someone! Trusting God's guiding hand to lead one of his chosen sons to be our groom, the last thing we need to do is go on a man hunt. God has got it handled.

We don't need to settle for a gorilla, no matter how great their banana mashed potatoes may taste. Our 'Author' is the best in the business, writing our love stories start to finish. The question is, do we trust Him with the pen?

Finding Your Prince

Paige Nicole Weslaski

Chapter 1:
Backstreet's Back, Alright!

"Show me the meaning of being lonely."
- Backstreet Boys

Looking up at the client, I saw his wavy blonde hair, his bright blue eyes, and his defined face. I had seen the face before many, many times. In fact, I had looked at this face every morning I woke up and every night I went to sleep for years, a poster of his face plastered directly next to my bed as a youngster. I'd stare at it hoping and praying someday I'd get lucky enough to see him in person.

Well, years later, my wish was granted. Standing before me was none other than Nick Carter: the '90's boy band heartthrob, looking even better than the poster.

It was my first day on the job working at the front desk of the Malibu Health Club, and of all people, the first person to walk in was Carter, my middle school dream man. I used to daydream of different scenarios of meeting him. I'd be in one of his concerts, front row, and he'd notice me in the crowd, pull me up on stage, and declare his immediate love for me.

Or, maybe we'd sit next to each other on a plane, I'd order a Ginger Ale, and he'd look at me with those dreamy eyes of his and whisper, "Ginger Ale is my favorite soda, will you be my wife?" In which I'd tell him I'd like to take things slow, and by slow I mean find the nearest chapel upon landing.

To my 12-year-old demise, neither ended up coming true, and I had forgotten all about my love for Carter until this moment. I immediately backtracked ten years, and all those love-y dove-y Backstreet Boy feelings came rushing back to my heart. Right in front of me. Nick CARTER!

It didn't go exactly how I would've wanted it to. He wasn't Prince Charming; he didn't gallop up on a white horse and sweep me off my feet and ride away into the sunset draping me in his arms like I would've preferred. Instead, he drudged into the health club to see one of the chiropractors about back pain, keeping his eyes straight ahead as I squeaked out a pathetic "hello."

After the longest thirty minutes of my life, he walked out of the doctors office and toward my desk to pay. "Holy moly, he's coming towards me. ME, of all people! Do I look okay? Can he see me sweating? Why didn't I curl my hair today? I knew I should have curled my hair!"

"Um, hello?" he asked.

Breathe in, breathe out, breathe in, breathe out. I could do this. Of course I could do this. All I had to do was slide his card. Why was I panicking? Why was I sweating?

"Nick Carter. I love you. I've always loved you. You're the one for me. My all. My everything. I know you don't know me, but I know everything about you! Backstreets back, alright! Remember that song? I do. I listened to it for hours and hours and hours..."

"Um, hello? Anybody there?"

Shaking my head, I realized I still hadn't said anything. "Uh, yeah, hi. It'll be fifty dollars exactly, sir."

Barely looking me in the eye, he handed me his American Express. I looked down at the card;

sure enough, NICK CARTER stamped in big silver letters. Trying to keep myself composed, I slid the card through the machine, hearing a beep: "declined," the machine read. Confused, I slid the card again, hearing the same beep.

"Nick, err, I mean, Mr. Carter, do you have any other cards I could charge?" With a loud sigh of frustration, he held out his Visa. Grabbing his card, our fingers touched, and it was magic. Sparks flew, trumpets sounded, and angels sang in Heaven. Did he feel it? He had to have felt it. It was electrifying. Paige Carter. I liked the sound of it. Would I have a small wedding or big wedding? What would my parents think? They'd probably freak out. Or what about those kids from high school? Why couldn't this have happened five years ago?

"Excuse me, can you let go of my hand?" he asked, annoyance in his voice.

"I think it was you holding my hand," I laughed. Ha. Ha. He didn't find it funny.

Awkwardly clearing my throat, I slid his new card, giving myself a mental pep-talk to pull myself together. And then, immediately after the swipe, it happened again. Declined.

How could Nick Carter's credit cards get declined? What was going on?

He groaned and rolled his eyes, telling me there was nothing wrong with his cards and blamed it on the machine.

Wow, he had great teeth. And what great style... wearing a loose fitting white V-neck. It's like he was trying to say "I know I'm hot, but I'm also trying to make it look natural." And boy, did it work. What. A. Hunk.

"Hello, miss? I think it's your machine?"

Abruptly jumping up, I backed away into the hallway.

Running to the file room, I started jumping up and down, tapping my boss on her shoulders. "He's here! My dream man! He's here! Nick! Nick Carter! You know, the gorgeous Backstreet Boy?! Backstreet's back!"

"Paige. Let me say this as clearly as I can. Get a hold of yourself! He comes in all the time! How can you expect to work here when you act like this! Plus you know he's engaged, right? Chill!"

"Well, he may be getting married, but we still had a moment." After explaining his card problems, she went out, fixed the machine, and saw him on his way.

Walking up to the balcony overlooking the parking lot, I watched him walk to his car, slide in, and back up to pull out of the lot. As he pulled away, he looked up at the windows, and I swear I saw him look up to me and give a head nod.

Walking to my desk, I patted myself on the back for handling it so swell. Sure, it could've gone better, but hey, I got a head nod! Nick and I had an understanding, obviously he was engaged and didn't want to stir up controversy with his fiance so he couldn't ask me on a date.

Our connection was as powerful as fireworks and he clearly didn't show his true affections towards me or he wouldn't have been able to control himself. My boss could tell me I was a nutcase as much as she wanted, but I knew the truth. I was Nick Carter's soulmate, and sooner or later he'd be back. Yeah, he'd be back all right.

Although I have yet to see Carter again, it doesn't phase me because I have someone who loves me that's even more special. Our Father in Heaven, the creator of the tree's and the ocean's and the star's and you and me, loves us so much that He never holds back His affection. God wants nothing more than a relationship with His children, asking us to spend time with Him to share our deepest thoughts and dreams and desires.

Now, let's say hypothetically all of my fourth grade wildest dreams had come true and Nick had asked me on a date right then and there. Would it have been wise for me to say yes? I mean, obviously I would have been honored and probably would have just stared at him like a goof until someone pinched me, but would it have been smart?

Truthfully, I don't know Nick's stance on faith. I don't know how he feels about God or attending church or serving as a role model. I don't know how seriously he looks to Christ as his savior.

"But Paige, this is Nick Carter we're talking about. Friends don't let friends turn down dates with Nick Carter."

Touché friend, but thinking about how much our God truly loves us, it's crucial to wait for a Godly man, no matter how handsome or famous or dreamy or... well, you get the picture.

So, Nick, if you're reading this, I'll have to decline. You're a great guy and all, and I know we hit it off quite nicely, but I'm going to pass on your silent yet obvious marriage proposal. My Father in Heaven already provides everything I need. But, if you call me up and sing "I Want it That Way," maybe, just maybe, I'd let you take me to church sometime. (wink, wink)

My encounter with Carter helped me see no matter how cool someone looks to the world, God sees their heart. God can do anything He wants; He could have made Nick fall in love with me at that specific moment if He wanted to! But would that have been best for me and my faith walk?

God is the world's absolute best matchmaker. He's even better than the love guru's on the hit show "Millionaire Matchmaker," plus He's free of charge! He knows who we're best suited for because He not only created us, but every guy in the whole world! We have nothing to fear when our God is near.

And, who knows, maybe God's just saving me for Nick's hunky brother Aaron? (half kidding)

Chapter 2:
Advice from a Recovering Heartbroken Heartbreaker

"No, sir, the girl really worth having won't wait for anybody." - F. Scott Fitzgerald

Now, you're probably reading this book thinking, "Who is this Paige chick and why does she think she's smart enough to write a book about finding a man? I mean, look at her, she's not even dating anyone! What a rip."

Right you are, beloved. I'm undoubtedly the worst person to write this book. As a middle and high schooler, I struggled with extreme insecurity, worried about my appearance and thinking people didn't like me. I thought I needed a boyfriend to prove myself and give myself an identity. A boyfriend would make me feel comfortable and accepted and adored and cherished, right? All my problems of insecurity would vanish, right?

Once I had my first kiss in eighth grade with a boy named Max, I was in for a pleasant surprise. My insecurity didn't clear up like I'd assumed, in fact, it FLARED up. It got worse than before! I was constantly checking my Motorola pink RAZR flip phone (very chic at the time) to see if he'd texted back. A minute would go by, then two minutes, and before I knew it, I had mentally broken up with him and taken him back seven times before receiving a response minutes later.

8th grade turned into 9th grade turned into 12th grade, and I went through boy after boy after boy.

I couldn't be single for the life of me. I needed a boyfriend because, well, I couldn't stand the thought of being alone! Not having a boyfriend meant no 'good morning beautiful' texts. It meant my self esteem would plummet! I was a ticking time bomb doing all I could to cover my emotions by having a boy at my hips. "If I'm never alone, I'll never have to face my insecurities," I figured.

I collected boyfriends the way Floyd Mayweather collects luxury cars. And I thought I had the perfect plan: I'd always feel wanted.

Thinking back, it was no wonder boys were talking to me with the lifestyle I was living: touching them on their arm every time I saw them, wearing the shortest of skirts, spending an hour on my hair and makeup, and starving myself for an attractive-looking body.

The reason I was asked to go on dates was not because I was special, it was because I was desperate and looking for love in any crook and cranny I could find. I was a lost, broken girl looking for acceptance. Acknowledgement from the male species was my drug, and I never quite felt complete.

High school turned into college, meaning one thing: freedom. Freedom to go out when I wanted, to hang out with anyone, to go anywhere, and to be my own person. The word "no" was not part of my vocabulary. I was down for any party - any adventure - any time. If someone wanted to go out, they could call me, I'd be there. There's a song titled "Young, Wild and Free" by Wiz Khalifa that served as one of my theme songs.

"So what we get drunk,

So what we smoke weed,
We're just having fun,
We don't care who see's.
So what we go out,
That's how it's supposed to be,
Living Young and Wild and Free."
(Emi Blackwood Music Inc.)

Except, I wasn't free. Once September of junior year rolled around, things started to shift. I started to feel weird about parties. I'd wake up the next morning feeling gross and bad about myself, and it wasn't just because of the hangover. My soul felt gross. A sorority sister of mine (shout out to Alpha Phi!) invited me to tag along to a chapel service on a Sunday night (after having been to a party the night beforehand, making a fool of myself).

Seeing kids (cool kids at that) willingly at church, raising their hands and praising God, the fog cleared in my head. I started to ask myself: "Am I actually free - going to these parties, dating anyone and everyone, and doing whatever I want? Or have the very things which promised freedom actually become my master?"

"Maybe these parties are causing my problems. Maybe that's why I'm feeling so crummy. I thought I was living 'Young, Wild, and Free,' but it's more like 'Young, Wild, and Enslaved!'"

Enslaved I was. Enslaved to my body image, enslaved to not wanting to miss out, and enslaved to thinking I needed boys to call me 'pretty' to know my worth. That very night, I made a decision. I would continue to live "Young, Wild, and Free," except now I'd really be free.

I met a man that night who put all the others from my past to shame. He blew my mind, opening my heart to what real love meant: Real love meant one person. Real love meant acceptance. Real love meant waiting. Real love meant trust.

I had never met anyone like him before, loving me just as I was, no questions asked. He knew about my broken past of serial dating, my insecurity, and my self-doubt.

And what did he do? While any decent man would have ran in the opposite direction, he sat with me while I cried to him. He even told me he wanted me to be his precious girl, not just for a day, or a week, but for my whole life.

Speechless, I was awe-struck. How could someone love me with all my baggage? How could someone sit with me for so long, telling me how worthy I was to him? How could someone accept me like this?

He knew he could help me change. He knew I was capable of far more than what I had done, and that I had potential to turn my life around, and even encourage others in the process!

I know exactly what you're thinking. "Who is this hunk and does he have a brother?"

The kind-hearted, loving, non-judgmental man was none other than Jesus Christ.

Maybe you've seen him on a stained glass window, or on a wooden cross at church, or on a necklace around your grandmother's neck.

I had seen him those places too, but I sure did not desire a relationship with a stained glass window. Because that's all He was, right? A man written about 2,000 years ago?

That night in the chapel, it became clear. No longer was Jesus a necklace around grandma's neck, He was a real person. So real, I knew with His help, I could do anything! I could quit partying, I could live as a single woman, and I could become secure in myself and my ability. I could live in freedom without the cobwebs of sin I had intertwined into my life. I could live in light, free of all the darkness I was used to.

No longer did I need a boyfriend. No longer did I need to flirt with every boy I met. No longer did I need to obsess over my appearance or what I said or did. I no longer had to please anybody but God! The scales fell off my eyes, and I was a new woman.

Allowing Him into my life led to lots of surprises. All the darkness I did my best to cover up was washed away through the blood of Christ. The kicker is - He asked me to change up a few things. In return, He gave me a clean, spacious, free life on a silver platter.

Do I regret sneaking out of my bedroom window, cheating on tests, and becoming a party animal? Partially, no. Of course, it led to lots of heartache and brokenness, but it also turned me into the woman I am today. A woman who knows the world has nothing to offer because I've tried it all. I've tried finding my worth in boys. I've tried taking lines of shots and smoking joints at parties. I've tried everything. Where did it leave me? Depressed, confused, and with a plummeted self-worth.

Do I still go out? Not the way I used to. Am I living young, wild, and free? Everyday. The

chains of this world have nothing on me
because I hold the key to unlock them all:
Jesus.

We are God's beloved, and He wants to lead us
down the perfect path He's predestined for us.
Our God has already hand-chosen the right
man for us: a man who will not only take good
care of us, but will point us to Christ every
single day.

God has a plan, He pinky promised in His word.
The stronger our grip holding His hand, the
less we'll have to worry. We don't need
someone in the short-term to be happy. We've
already got Someone's hand to hold, and He
doesn't plan on letting go.

Chapter 3:
We are Not Commodities

"Too many young girls have eating disorders due to low self-esteem and distorted body image. I think it's so important for girls to love themselves and to treat their bodies respectfully."
- Ariana Grande

Sophomore year of college, I was far from emotionally stable. I was falling short in the self-confidence arena, trying to make up for it with my looks. The idea of a guy not finding me attractive was personally alarming; I was desperate for love from others because my self-love tank was dangerously empty.

I wanted to do everything in my power to look outwardly beautiful. I was ridiculously thin and my boobs were generally nonexistent (after months of eating air for breakfast), but nothing Victoria's Secret couldn't help. The one thing I was lacking? A Barbie button nose.

I had harnessed a complex about my nose since middle school. As if middle school wasn't hard enough, I'd look at myself in the mirror thinking no one could possibly like someone with my nose. For my 8th grade graduation, I unsuccessfully asked my parents for a nose job.

"Paige, honey, you're too young for that! Maybe when you're older, okay?"

Shoulders slumped, I held onto that hope.

7 years later, I wanted it more than ever. I wanted sex-appeal, and a bump on my nose was sure not going to stand in my way.

Living in California for college, I called my dad back in Wisconsin a few days before my birthday. "Dad, I've thought about it long and hard. I'm an adult now, and I want the surgery."

After a long silence, he quietly responded, "Well, let's have a doctor consultation and go from there."

Mouth hitting the floor, I had no words. "Wait, what? Really? Seriously?!"

"Set it up and I'll fly out in a few weeks."

Researching the best plastic surgeons in Beverly Hills, Dr. K was the obvious choice. He was a big-shot amongst all the celebrities, Playboy bunnies in particular.

A few of my friends from college had gotten plastic surgery before, to which they told me the pain was minuscule compared to the awesome long-term results. "Get ready for a brand new you," my friend told me. Quite the statement, eh?

Walking into Dr. K's office, the waiting room was decorated with blinding chrome and bright purple furniture, pictures of topless women with signatures ("thank you Dr. K!") draping the walls, and club music blaring through the speakers hidden in a gaudy plant. We were approached by the thinnest woman I had ever seen in my life, asking us to take a seat. Flipping through some magazines, my dad and I exchanged nervous glances.

Dr. K poked his head from the hallway and motioned us to follow. Sitting in the consultation room, the doctor looked bored, asking what we needed to know.

"Um, well, could you explain your procedure?" I asked. (I mean obviously, right?)

Grabbing a piece of blank computer paper, Dr. K drew a circle, which he said was my head, and a sideways V - with a squiggle in the middle - indicating my nose. He then drew a line through the squiggle, saying the procedure would get rid of my nose bump.

"Um, okay, yeah, that wasn't exactly rocket science. Don't you guys take pictures of her and show us over a computer what it would look like post-op?" my dad questioned.

"Eh, no. We do that sometimes, but I've got a surgery to get to. Peace!" Handing me the doodle, he was gone.

Heading to his assistant's office, of whom was just as thin as the receptionist, we were given the price-tag: $8,000, often more depending on complications.

"Well, hun. It's expensive, and I don't necessarily feel comfortable with this place, but it's your birthday and we could always get someone else. It's your body, and it's your life.

You know your mom and I love you no matter what."

Telling the assistant we didn't in fact want the appointment that had opened up for later that day, we walked out of the office. I told my dad I had a lot to think about. And boy oh boy, did I ever.

I wanted it, of course. I wanted to be pretty. I wanted to be liked. I wanted to be a Barbie. But deep in my gut, something felt off. Having met that doctor, of whom I did not necessarily trust, I couldn't picture myself getting it done, at least not in the coming months.

Calling my dad a week later, I shared the news: "I decided - and I can't even believe I'm saying this - but I don't want it. I don't want a nose job."

Breathing a heavy sigh of relief, he congratulated me, telling me my heart had never looked more beautiful.

Funny, in middle-school, the worst part about looking in the mirror was seeing my nose. Today, washing my hands at Starbucks, I glanced at myself in the mirror. The one difference? My nose was my favorite part about looking in the mirror.

I may not have the cute bunny-slope curved nose I envied for so many years, but I'm beautiful, just like you. We're "beautifully and wonderfully made" in the image of God, made exactly how He wants us. He placed us here for one reason: to glorify Him by serving and loving those around us. How can we do that when we're self-absorbed in our personal appearance?

Looking back, I was the ugliest version of myself sophomore year. Helping others was nowhere on my radar. I was completely focused on my exterior, ignoring the needs of my friends and peers, constantly fishing for compliments.

Before making major decisions like plastic surgery, we need to ask ourselves: "Will this help us or hurt us in the long run? Will it help benefit our testimony to point others to the Creator of the world? Or will it make us more self-obsessed than ever?"

We often think we need something we don't yet have in order to be worthy. Whether it's a nose job, lips like Kylie Jenner, a rose gold Michael Kors watch, a Hermes Birkin bag, a french manicure, or eyelash extensions.

Nothing can fill the 'gap' in our heart like Jesus can (even a thigh 'gap')!

How do we want our future daughters to feel about themselves? Embarrassed? Ugly? Worthless? Like no one could ever love them? Its the same with Jesus, it hurts Him seeing how insecure we feel.

Just last night I watched the last ten minutes of 'The Bachelorette' and thought, "Goodness, I could never have twenty guys all pursuing me, I'm not special enough!"

I know I'm not alone in this arena. All of us, guys and gals, tall and short, freckles and dimples, have personal doubts about our appearance and abilities - often on a daily basis.

That's not how God originally designed us to live. When God gave Adam and Eve the garden of Eden, they roamed freely without any clothes on. At the time, it was no big deal because they had nothing to be anxious, self-conscious, or worried about. Once they sinned, they immediately started to make clothes for themselves because they felt embarrassed.

"Okay now Paige, I'm not about to prance around naked like Adam and Eve."

Trust me, both the police and I agree. But, God sees us as flawless, without a thing to feel self-conscious about. Once we start to ignore His Word, we immediately believe the lies of our culture, thinking we need to look and act a specific way. We were created to live lives of freedom, excitement, joy, and self-worth. God did not create us to think we are doormats.

Audrey Hepburn, arguably the most chic woman to ever live, once said "happy girls are the prettiest."

As God's princesses, let's follow her advice and live like the happiest girls this world's ever seen. Let's prove the world wrong, smiling when it tells us to frown and throwing those goofy gossip mags in the trash where they belong. Next time we feel unworthy, let's stop, drop, and read the Good News: Jesus sees us as so beautiful, He wants to be our true love.

We're only human, and I realize it's easier said than done. A few months ago, one of my best friends met me for lunch at Casa Del Mar's pool in Santa Monica. Sitting on cozy chairs in a quiet corner overlooking the Pacific waves crashing onto the sand, we enjoyed an appetizer of fish tacos and drank green smoothies, talking the afternoon away.

This particular friend of mine has been brimming with confidence from day one. She has a similar background to me, as we both dabbled in the party scene and dated a small army of guys we knew weren't good for us before finding our faith.

As I took my first bite of a Mahi Mahi and avocado taco, my friend said something strange.

"I sometimes feel like no one could ever love me."

My eyes as big as my plate, I couldn't help but cough out, "Wait, what?"

If I were a man, this gal would be the prototype I was looking for: beautiful, helpful, encouraging, prayerful, and servant-like. Digging deeper, she explained how she often feels pangs of insecurity, unknowingly wondering if God really had someone for her.

She is not alone. I have had seasons when I've felt pretty crummy, too. "I feel ugly, how could anyone love someone who looks like me? I'm awkward, how could someone stand marrying me? I'm so clumsy, lazy, etc."

We are not worthless. According to the Life Handbook we've graciously been given by the world's Creator, we are enough, we are beloved, and we are worthy.

God does not create junk. Those who take His hand and walk down the path of His grace have nothing to fear, least of all thinking a man can't someday love them. Let's forget about fad diets, obsessive calorie counting, or needing to look a certain way. God is the ultimate Matchmaker and will, in His timing, give us the right person who finds us lovely.

In the meantime, how are we ladies of faith to act? With elegance. Inward elegance, that is. Inward elegance will never fade, unlike our youth or beauty.

Let's be women of truth who stick to our word. Let's be women of confidence, standing by the quote "there's great power in knowing we have it." Let's be God-fearing women, knowing our ultimate path in life is destined and determined through our faith in Jesus Christ, the ultimate Romancer. Let's be women of love, pouring our God-given gifts into those around us, knowing we were born with specific talents others may lack.

Let's not be afraid to turn someone down because we aren't afraid of singleness. Let's be women of grace, poise, elegance, charm, and dignity. Let's act as women of true beauty, found in the heart, and ignore those who don't help us shine.

There's nothing wrong with us being the one who got away. Nothing good can happen after midnight - think Cinderella - let's keep those boys wanting more.

Let's ignore our stumbles and keep our chins up high. Let's look up at the stars, not down at our feet.

We are women of purity, modern luxury, and sophistication. We are not a piece of candy. We are worth more than our exterior and don't need to settle for a man who doesn't agree.

We are under attack. We see 10,000 advertisements a day without even realizing it, most of which are poison for the soul. The devil, a loser who knows he won't spend eternity with us in Heaven, wants to make our lives miserable by feeding us lies. But thankfully, we're stronger than him because we have Christ in us. We have the power to ignore the 'liar of all liars' by knowing our real treasure lies not in our appearance or a man, but in Heaven.

We are not a car in a parking lot to get chosen. We choose a man just as much as he chooses us. We are not something to be used and traded in. As long as we trust in the sovereignty of Jesus, we can rest assured our insecurity over finding a man will drive off into the sunset without us.

Chapter 4:
Waving Goodbye to the Ex

"Everyone has had a bully or mean girl or ex-boyfriend who has tried to bring them down."
- Demi Lovato

Have you seen the movie 'He's Just Not that Into You?' It's one of those movies everyone pretends to love but secretly hates because it makes them feel a little insecure. The basic premise of the movie follows different couples in New York City, all boiling down to one person within the couple feeling rejected by the other.

The movie came out the summer of my sophomore year of high school. I remember competing at a championship swim meet in Milwaukee with my teammates at the time. I was dating a swimmer from another team, and we both qualified for finals, meaning we had a few hours to kill after the preliminary session. We decided to go to the movie theater and settled on 'He's Just Not that Into You.'

The ironic part about the story is we weren't doing very well in our relationship. We didn't see each other often, and I (being a wee immature) was insecure about where we stood. He had stopped calling as often and didn't text me every morning like he used to. I was starting to get nervous.

I was looking forward to the movie. This would be our chance to rekindle our flame! Maybe, after spending some time together, he'd remember how incredibly irresistable I was and everything would go back to normal!

It didn't pan out that way. We watched the movie without a single hand-hold. We barely said a word to each other, keeping our eyes glued to the screen of the movie describing our fate. He just wasn't that into me anymore!

As you can guess, our relationship dwindled to nothing. We stopped talking all-together and saw each other only on rare unplanned occasions, all of which were awkward.

Did I walk away from the relationship like I should have? No. By the looks of it, I was over him. But because of my pride, I was crushed, confused, and plotting how to win him back.

"Maybe... if I see him at a swim meet... I can make sure I look really cute and trip over his bag and he'll catch me and we'll live happily ever after!"

But after a few failed attempts of 'just happening' to see him with full hair and makeup, I knew it was useless. He started dating someone else, and I was alone.

As a hopeless romantic, I felt embarrassed and confused. "Why did he break up with me? What was the deal? What do I do now?"

Before we even stepped into the theater, I knew he wasn't all that into me. For about a month prior, I could feel it. I was no longer being pursued, I was doing the pursuing. But instead of recognizing his disinterest, I ignored it, thinking he needed to hear more from me in order to bring him back to the "honeymoon" stage.

That did nothing but push him away further because the roles had been switched. Instead of letting the man be the man and call me, I started calling him.

There are lots and lots of fish in the sea. That means there's at least one who will treasure and adore us. But it also means there's at least one who will never want to be with us.

The trouble with our society is falling for the fish who don't want us. We want to change their minds and prove to them how worthy we are, when in reality we're (usually) in for nothing but disappointment and self-inflicted anguish.

There will always be someone out there who doesn't want us. It doesn't matter who we are, whether we're Megan Fox or Selena Gomez or Taylor Swift. It's interesting, too, thinking about the "love lives" of beautiful celebrities. Swift, for example, had a fling with John Mayer only to get her feelings hurt. She probably knew he was trouble when he walked in, but wanted a challenge. Even with millions of men dying to be her one and only, she chose someone she knew would make it a game. Someone to whom she had to prove herself.

Am I recommending all girls date as often as I did, or at all? No. But once it's the right man, we'll know it. When we meet our Mr. Right, expecting him to 'step up and be a man' will keep gender roles in the right place. Instead of taking the man's role, us women can sit back and wait (while remaining kind and approachable) to allow God to work.

I love hearing stories of how old couples met. They usually sound something like "he saw me at the fair, climbed the ferris wheel, and wouldn't get down until I told him I'd go out with him." (or is that just 'The Notebook?') Most old love stories sound the same: boy met girl, boy asked girl to date, boy asked girl to marry. That's why many old couples are still happily together!

The problem with our generation is that ladies confuse themselves as being the leader in the relationship.

"He never comes up with good dates so I plan them all. He doesn't ever text me so I text him. He doesn't like being in a relationship on Facebook so I just post all over his wall so girls get the picture he's mine."

If I were a boy, I know exactly how I would want things done. I'd want to pursue a woman and treat her like a princess. I'd choose the restaurants and make decisions. And that's exactly how, deep down, almost all men think.

Even if they play things off as "liking when women ask them out," I'd assume deep down they'd rather do the pursuing. Women do not need to elbow their way through.

If he doesn't call, he is not interested. If a man is truly interested in a woman, there's only about a 1 in 1,000 chance he'll lose her number or be too busy to contact her. That boy was no longer interested in me, and instead of accepting it, I made things worse.

Allowing ourselves to fall for someone who's not into us is detrimental. We're worth far more than that, beloved. Trusting in God's almighty power, we can ignore those who ignore us. If we know he's trouble, we shouldn't give him the time of day, babe. Let's learn from my mistakes… and Taylor's song.

"A man who finds a wife finds a good thing." (Proverbs 18:22) Notice, the verse does not say 'a woman who finds a man finds a good thing.' We do not need to search, we can instead wait to be found, knowing we're someone's 'good thing.'

The idea of 'ignoring those who ignore us' was tough for me to fathom. Moving to Malibu, California my sophomore year of college, I was aware I may have a run-in or two with some celebrities.

A few weeks into school, my new friends and I went to a hotspot, Cafe Habana. Cafe Habana is a Mexican restaurant that turns into a bar/dance club come night-time. This particular night, the place was packed; there was an up-and-coming DJ and lots of dancing.

Leaning over the bar trying to get the bartender's attention, I noticed brown, wispy hair on the man's head next to me. "Wow, he's cute," I thought. "How do I know that guy? Is he in my science class?"

In a matter of moments, it hit me: I was standing next to a major celebrity, the man I used to watch on a hit MTV reality show. The very man I had been crushing over via television was trying to order a vodka soda... standing right next to me. (I unfortunately can't share his name - herein referred to as Bryan)

I needed to talk to him. He had always been such a gentleman to the women on the show!

"Are you Bryan?" I blurted out. (smooth, Paige)

"Hmm," he said. "Who's Bryan? Definitely not me. I'm not Bryan, whoever that is."

Unsure if he was being rude or playful, I teased back. "Um, yeah you definitely are. I used to watch your show!" Again, very smooth.

"Nope. I'm not Bryan. Who's Bryan? That's a funny name, don't you think?"

Paying the bartender, I looked his way once more. "Nice meeting you, Bryan."

"See ya, sweetie," he winked.

A few weeks after the initial encounter, I saw Bryan again at a coffee shop. "Hi!" I squealed as he walked off with his mocha latte. "Um, hi?" he said. Another moment, almost as great as the first one, I thought. (delusional, I understand)

Throughout my sophomore year, I saw him a couple more times, buying a smoothie at the Vitamin Barn, eating brunch at Coogies, and munching on a sandwich at John's Garden. Each time I would overplay the interaction (if anything at all) we shared.

Once he held the door open for me at a restaurant and I melted, thinking we were destined to be together. Another time, he smiled at me at the mall, and it was solidified in my mind: he was totally into me and we would grow old together and I could move into his Malibu beach pad and I could become besties with his famous sisters and, and, and…

I had quite the imagination. I was not secure with myself, and I was constantly looking for attention and reassurance from boys, even celebrities who didn't know my name. My junior and senior years of college, I'd still see him around here and there, except at that point he was dating a cute blonde whom was always at his side.

It was safe to say I was no longer crushing on Bryan. I was becoming more comfortable in my own skin and grown more realistic in my thought process, finally allowing my heart and mind to be shaped by Jesus Christ.

As women, it's easy to project a specific image on a man we wish was real. Funny as the story is, I left my first encounter with Bryan thinking, "Wow! What a real gentleman." In reality, he hadn't been very nice to me. Pretty rude, in fact.

My little encounters with Bryan are pathetic. But it's a prime example of how women often run after men, make the first move, compromise themselves, and over-exaggerate scenarios.

Bryan and I were never friends, and I would be highly surprised if he could pick me out in a line of ten girls. But the premise of the story is pretty similar to my actual ex-boyfriends. I'd overplay situations, we'd break up, all my hopes and dreams would come crashing down, and I'd walk away more bruised than before.

Throughout my lifetime, I have dated a handful of guys, some first-class men, others not. But looking back, I find it pretty wacky I would stay with someone who treated me badly, dated other girls at the same time, put me down, or talked badly about me.

As an insecure teenager, it seemed those guys, the ones who weren't Prince Charmings, were the one's I ran after most. I wanted to prove to myself I was worthy by "winning their love," choosing bad-boys over guys who would have actually been gentlemen.

My word of advice is not to settle for someone who doesn't treat us like a princess. There is nothing - I repeat - nothing wrong with being single. In fact, singleness is the most beautiful time of a girls life. It's a time for us to soul search, to grow into the women we want to be, and to not compromise ourselves to fit a certain mold of what a specific man is looking for.

I recommend we take time to figure out who we are, and only then look for the one we're compatible with. Changing who we are is not something we need to do. I guarantee there's a man out there, celebrity or not, who would be lucky to have any of us. Not for who we can pretend to be, but our real selves. We don't want a man to fall in love with our 'false selves' only to be shocked when the 'real us' shows up!

Accepting Christ, we are no longer classified by our past decisions. As young ladies, we can let a break-up 'break us' or we can let it bring us closer to God. Jesus didn't save us from a broken life to watch us date someone who would take us back to where we came from.

Whenever I see an ex-boyfriend, they mention how I've changed, and they couldn't be more right. I have changed! I'm no longer serving to entertain their hormones because my eyes aren't on them, they're on Christ.

We are all going to die someday and not come back. Consequently, we are not on this Earth to worship an ex. Let's stop going back to what hurts us. God has someone better for us. We do not need to beg, crawl, manipulate, or convince anyone to be with us. The secret to detaching from an ex is attaching to Christ. Let's not allow someone to steal our sunshine. And we definitely don't want someone we have to convince to go to church!

If an ex is messaging us, we need to distinguish when it's time to retreat. Is the ex actually worth responding to? Or should we just block their number and keep well on our merry way?

God gives wisdom to those who ask for a spirit of discernment, and as His daughters, we should pray for that wisdom.

Let's forgive those who hurt us and choose our paths wisely. We are gems, no matter what anyone says, beloved. Bright, shining gems with a grand future ahead.

Sayonara, exes.

Chapter 5:
Instead of Looking for Somebody, Become Somebody

"I recommend to all my friends that they be alone for a while. When you're in love, or dating someone, you filter your life decisions through their eyes. When you spend a few years being who you are, completely unbiased, you can figure out what you actually want."
- Taylor Swift

If you told any of my friends from highschool I'd be solo-dolo in my early twenties for three years straight, I know exactly how they'd respond:

"You must be nuts."

They were all aware of my boy obsession, and I doubt a single one could have predicted my future. Becoming a Christian turned my life upside-down.

Going into my junior year of college, I thought I had a lot going for me. I was stick-thin, a member of Pepperdine's division 1 swim team and the Alpha Phi sorority, and I dated the "love of my life," or so I thought.

He was everything I wanted in a man. He was tall, dark, handsome, and hit everything on my "future hubby" checklist. He was born and raised in Los Angeles, where his father was a Hollywood producer, so he knew the area well, taking me on fun dates around the city. We ate ice cream sandwiches at the infamous Diddy Riese, rode the roller coaster on the Santa Monica pier, and star-gazed on Zuma Beach. I thought he could be the one.

He drove a brand-new Mercedes, one afternoon driving us up into the Hollywood Hills to see the view of the city. We parked at the tip-top and started walking hand-in-hand as he pointed out which houses his family owned. There were more than ten.

Needless to say, I didn't foresee myself ending things with him. Ever. Why would I? He was handsome, he came from a good family, he was wealthy, and he adored me. I didn't see a glitch in our future together. We could have a big fancy wedding, he could take over his dad's company as a producer, and I could be a stay-at-home mom in the Hills. What more could I possibly need, right?

That is, until the night in the chapel when everything changed. I took a step away from myself to see if I was actually happy. I should have been happy, right? What more could a girl want?

I realized I wasn't living the life I really wanted. I was sick of mercilessly counting calories for a stick-thin body, I was sick of the glitz of the parties, and I was sick of dating someone (and sleeping with someone) when I knew I needed a time of singleness.

I left the chapel, drove straight to his apartment, and ended things, tears in both our eyes. He was the man I wanted to marry, but I knew God felt otherwise. I knew I needed, for the first time in years, to walk away from the dating scene to fall in love with God.

It has not been easy. Some days have sucked. I've struggled thinking my standards are too high; that the man I'm waiting for doesn't exist. I've thought maybe I should cross a few things off my mental 'non-negotiables' list.

"Maybe he doesn't have to love Jesus. Maybe he doesn't have to treat his mother with respect. Maybe he doesn't need to have a passion, or a bright future, or a solid group of friends."

But we've got to trust God has a plan.

Sure, easier said than done, right? What about watching all our friends date around?

As long as we've allowed Jesus into our hearts, He is guiding our path, which He personalized to fit our specific journey.

Being as single as a dollar bill, I've been learning to be creative with my free time. This single season is a time for:

1. Growing in Our Passions
A man once told me his main attraction toward women was their level of passion. "I don't care if her passion is mowing the lawn, I want a woman that loves doing something, anything!" There's no better time to get involved in a youth group, to learn to golf, to take painting or ballet lessons, or to start a book or old movie club.

2. Becoming daddy's little girl again

Since I'm currently living back at home, I've been spending lots of time with my mom, dad, and brother. We'll be married the rest of our lives, and singleness is the perfect time to squeeze in every bit of family bonding we can.

3. Deleting the ex's digits

I recently watched the movie 'The Holiday' about two couples who meet and fall in love. The best part of the movie is when actress Kate Winslet tells her ex-beau Jasper to get out of her house and life. Likewise, we are not our past, so why not let 'em go for good?

4. Reading the novel 'God on a Harley'

Feeling broken and alone, the narrator found Christ (on a Harley, hence the title) and He helped her rebuild her life, soon finding a man much better than she could have imagined.

5. Remembering: we are not chewbacca

We have nothing to fear about finding a future mate because God is in control. There's lads out there looking for ladies just like us. While others are hiring dating coaches and using online services, we can feel peace knowing we've hired the best Matchmaker of all - God.

We can grow into the mature women God has called us to be. In the eyes of the living God, we are precious gems, worthy of nothing but His very best.

As His daughters, we have a reason to keep our heads up because we are strong, independent women with a future as bright as our smiles and our faith. Instead of sweating over looking for love, we can let love find us.

Personally, I've found the most effective way of figuring out who I want to be is to find role models. One of which being my mom-siccle.

She is the fittest woman I know. Competing in running races and Ironman triathlons, she runs, bikes, and swims regularly to stay in tip-top shape.

That being said, I asked my mom to wake me up early one morning to join her on her weekly Saturday morning trail run.

7 AM, she woke me up, and I told her I had changed my mind. "Yeah, mom, I think I'm good on the whole running thing. I would go but I'm actually really busy," I groggily whispered as I sunk my head back into the pillow.

"Fine, you'll miss out on all the fun then, missy!" Ugh.

I reluctantly got up, slammed a coffee, and told her I was in. But that I would only run for half. Or a quarter. Or a block. Motivation at its finest, I'm aware.

I made it more than a block, so that was a good sign. As we passed by the river bank, I popped out my earbud and asked her how she motivated herself everyday.

Running a few steps in silence, she told me I was going to laugh. Chuckling, I was confused. "Wait, what? Why?" Running a bit more, she started to explain:

"Remember that Sims game you played when you were young? Well, if you were controlling a Sims character, and they were supposed to represent you and your life, what would you have them do? Would you have ran this morning or stayed in bed?"

"You can use it in any aspect of life. What you do with your time, what you eat, who you hang out with, how hard you work… Don't focus so much on the pain of running or having to work hard at something, look instead at the bigger picture of making yourself the best you can be."

I was impressed. "Another analogy I use is from the movie Rocky," she said, hopping over a turtle.

"What's that?"

"When Rocky's facing Apollo Creed in the boxing ring, he says he just wants to go the distance. He wants to make it through as many rounds as he can."

"It doesn't matter how fast we run, as long as we go the distance. It doesn't matter how long it takes us to do something as long as we're trying. Taking the first step is always the hardest part. We just gotta go out there and do it!"

I couldn't have been happier I ran that morning.

We only live this life once before we spend eternity with Jesus in Heaven, and it's up to us what we do with it. I saw a quote once, it went like this:

"JUST DO IT, later. There's no rush. Have a snack instead. Maybe a nap, too. Seriously, just take it easy. Take a load off, buddy. You earned it. Eat the whole cake. The whole darn thing."

Rest and cake are good. Very good, in fact. But reaching our goals and making the world a better place? It takes time, hard work, and consistency. There's no doubt my mom sometimes wants to skip a day or two, but with her two quirky mindsets: living life like a Sims character and 'going the distance' like Rocky Balboa, she knows the end prize far outweighs the short-term discomfort.

My mom's advice was wonderful, but it doesn't beat the advice from my late grandmother. She never left the house without her pearls, a spritz of Chanel 'Number 5' perfume, and a custom blazer jumpsuit. She was the most sophisticated woman I had ever met, and the gifts she gave me were out of this world: A beautiful quartz gem ring, a hand-made mink hat, and hand-stitched fur gloves. Classy chic at its finest.

Since her funeral, I've been slowly blowing dust off boxes of her belongings. I've found old classic novels she used to read, 'Jane Eyre' and 'Wuthering Heights' being her favorites, bound in gold-lined paper. I opened a bronze jewelry box to find countless rings and earrings. And I found a couple of old scrapbooks. Flipping through one of those scrapbooks, I came across a story she wrote when she was merely eight years old.

"Once upon a time, the noisiest place in the world was a city called Hub-Bub. The people of Hub-Bub never talked, they only yelled. They were very proud that their ducks were the quackiest, their doors the slammiest, and their police whistles the shrilliest in the whole wide world. But I wouldn't want to live in Hub-Bub."

The funny thing is, reading the poem helped me realize how much she hadn't changed from a young girl to an old woman. My grandmother never left her small town of Ripon, Wisconsin of only 7,000 people. Other than occasional vacations, she never lived anywhere else.

Right before her passing, I asked if she had any regrets staying in one place. I asked if she ever got bored, if the town got dull, or if the people grew stale.

"Paige, baby, everything I loved was right here. My husband, my children, my childhood friends, my favorite book stores, my favorite downtown coffee shops. I love how the snow glimmers in the sun on the hill at Ripon College, and the feeling of long afternoons boating on the lake in the summertime."

"There's nothing I'm more thankful for than planting my roots in this quiet town. It gave me room to think, friends for life, and took away the pressures of living. It was easy, honey."

"Sometimes, life isn't about far-off adventures. It's about simple pleasures; inviting your next door neighbor for tea, scones, and Bridge; sipping cold drinks on the pontoon; meeting your best friends for brunch. Don't worry about the hustle-and-bustle of what the world tells you is supposed to be fun, pleasurable, or exciting. Usually, the most treasured things in life are the simplest."

I was blown away. She didn't find it important to follow passing trends, she stuck to what she knew best: loving her family, wearing her pearls, and enjoying the small pleasures of small town living.

One of my favorite things about my grandmother was her love for the classics. Classic movies, classic clothes, classic novels, and classic music. She wasn't one for loud, obnoxious things in life; her life was too full of lovely treasures.

Do we find ourselves liking certain trends or following certain rules because of the posts on our Facebook feed? Are the shows we're watching affecting our ideas on life? What about the music we listen to or the magazines we read?

My advice, courtesy of the world's classiest grandmother:

If it makes your head hurt, don't do it. If it gives you anxiety, don't listen to it. If it makes you self-conscious, don't read it. If they hurt your feelings, don't hang out with them. If it degrades your beliefs, don't watch it.

Life goes fast. A few months ago I was chatting with my grandmother over gingersnap cookies and cocoa, and now she's in Heaven. But she lived life to the fullest. Not based on the world's perceptions, but based on her own. As an 8-year-old, she knew big city living wasn't for her, and she respected that her whole life. She ruled her own life and pursued her childhood plans.

Her story makes me think: What's important to me? What kind of life do I want? While the world tells me I need to fit into a specific mold to be cool or trendy, I want to be… me. I want to dive into my personal passions regardless of what others think.

Growing up, we're taught to be and act a certain way. Listening to authority, sitting still when we're told, following direction; children are (to a point) forced to squeeze their creativity into a pre-shaped box.

Because of those strict boundaries from childhood, many grown adults don't uncover their true passions for fear of becoming a social outcast. They're nervous to swim upstream while everyone else swims downstream. They shiver at the thought of dancing to a different beat and facing criticism or exclusion.

To excel at something, one must deviate from the crowd and do things normal people don't do. Michael Jordan played five hours of basketball a day. Eminem sat through middle and high school scribbling rhymes to every word he could think of in over 100 notebooks. Justin Bieber sang for tips on the side of the street as an 11 year old kid. Normal people don't do those things.

At the time, it made them a little weird and different. But that's exactly what gave them an edge.

Jimmy Kimmel of the 'Tonight Show' wasn't the best student as a youngster, often getting in trouble in class for, you guessed it, joking around. Instead of quenching his light, he decided to shine even brighter, strengthening his comedic nature and becoming a professional jokester, exactly what his teachers told him he could never do.

Instead of trying to fit in, we should rather try to become the 'right fit.' The 'right fit' meaning who we are at our core. Instead of tirelessly trying to change, we should instead embrace our uniqueness and become more of the wacky, lame, hilarious, joyful, go-big-or-go-home humans God uniquely created us to be.

The leaning tower of Pisa was built with an incorrect foundation leading to a crooked architectural framework. In the 1930's, Mussolini saw the tower as a sign of Italy's weakness and ordered for its straightening. The architects couldn't complete the job without damaging the building, so it's still leaning today.

Little do people know, there's a massive cathedral built beautifully right next to the tower, yet no one travels to Pisa to see that building. They come for the tower because it's different, unique, and tilted.

How are we tilted? What has the world tried to "straighten out" in our lives? Is it our dedication to a sport? The way we dress? The locations we travel to? Our faith in God?

My favorite story in the Bible is the story of David. A young, small shepherd boy, David visited the camp of a major battle scene because his father instructed him to bring food to his older brothers (trained soldiers on the battle line). The entire camp was distraught over not being able to kill Goliath, the prized fighter and leader of the opposing team.

Little David decided to take his wooden slingshot without any armor or backup and grabbed a tiny stone to sling at Goliath, of whom was hysterically laughing at baby David. The stone hit Goliath right between the eyes and knocked him cold. David then skipped up to the unconscious Goliath and killed him with his own sword.

None of the trained warriors could kill Goliath, yet a small shepherd boy used what others saw as a measly toy to defeat the enemy; a toy David happened to be well-practiced and skilled at.

Are people laughing at us for trying something different? Are armored soldiers shaking their heads as we practice shooting our slingshot?

Let's be us, honeybee. The very best, over-the-top, extra chocolatey-sprinkles people only we can be! We can wave to the world's clones as they all march past in place. We can paint bright colors, sing funny songs, skip instead of walk, say yes instead of no, and be us! It's contagious and we'll be respected for our uniqueness.

Chapter 6:
Why Your Weirdness is Actually... Normal

"You only live once and life is wonderful, so eat the darn red velvet cupcake." – Emma Stone

Growing up, I worried I was too different. I'd notice myself doing things others didn't do. I didn't know what my deal was! "Why do I feel a need to sneak off from big crowds for a moment alone? Why do I daydream about my future more than living in the present? Why do I come up with grand future plans, only to have a different plan the very next day?"

None of it made sense until I completed a Myer's Briggs personality test in college. Professor Selby of Leadership 101 explained to the class how the results would give us a much grander view of ourselves.

Taking the test was more fun than I anticipated: 'Do you feel a constant need for something new? Do people make you energized or exhausted? Do you daydream and forget what you're doing? Do you enjoy alone time? How do you feel speaking in front of others? Are you a planner on vacations, or do you go-with-the-flow?'

The following class, Professor Selby gave us each a hefty packet based on our personality type. Opening my packet, it said 'INFP - the Dreamer.'

After reading through the first pages, I was impressed at its accuracy. INFP's have an ingrained desire to figure out their life's purpose, and they do best working as writers (go figure!), actors, pastors, counselors, and art teachers. They make up 4% of the population, and others included Audrey Hepburn, Princess Diana, Johnny Depp, and Isabell Briggs Myers (the creator of the test).

Reading through the description, it said "INFPs are creative, idealist loners." I knew I should have been offended, but I totally am a loner sometimes and always wondered why I sort of liked it that way.

Professor Selby had us break up into two groups: introverts and extroverts, based on the results. Out of all thirty students, only three of us were introverts. Lo and behold, I was the only INFP in class.

The packet helped me understand why I'm different from other people. I like my alone time, others get energized from being around big groups. I like doing things my own way, others like rules to follow. I like daydreaming and asking questions, others like to live in the moment.

It's wonderful how different we all are. God says "all the hairs on our heads are numbered" (Matthew 10:30). God has a special plan for us no one else can do.

I lived my whole life hating the fact I daydreamed so often and had to sneak away from big crowds. I didn't realize I was created that way for a purpose!

Not being tied down is one of the most beautiful times of a woman's life; it's a time of self-discovery, self-love, and inner peace. Going on dates with God, we can allow the right man to find us while we're doing something we love!

I once asked a guy friend of mine why he was still single. He was in his mid-twenties, very cute, and was working on his masters at Pepperdine. He told me he was soaking up his singleness and enjoying it! He told me he loved doing things on his own: going to see movies, biking along the Santa Monica boardwalk, and playing basketball.

He recommended I do the same to figure out precisely who I am and what I like to do; to not rush into anything that wasn't for me. That way, I'd know what to look for in a future mate.

I understood his advice for myself sitting in a conference room at MTV's central offices.

My junior year of college, I desperately wanted to intern at MTV. Living in Malibu, the MTV headquarters were located in downtown Santa Monica, a short drive down Pacific Coast Highway from the Pepperdine campus.

On a whim, I applied through the MTV website, sending my resume and cover letter not thinking I'd get a response. The very next day, I received a call from an unknown number between classes.

Nonchalantly answering, I was in for a surprise.

"Hi, this is the VP of marketing at MTV. We've received your resume and think you'd be a great fit. Can you be here in 30 minutes for an interview?"

"Um, yeah totally! I'll leave right now!" Skipping my second class, I ran to my apartment, changed into heels, a long dress, and a blazer, and hopped into my car.

Stepping into the elevator off the underground parking structure, I noticed how each floor housed the offices of different television channels all owned by Viacom. Level one indicated the BET offices, level two was CMT, and three was Comedy Central.

As I passed through Nick Jr, Nickelodeon, Nick@Nite, Spike, MTV2, and VH1, I finally hit the top floor: MTV. As the elevator door opened, I felt I had stepped into Disneyland. A decorated airstream trailer welcomed me into the offices, as well as surfboards and streamers hanging from the ceilings. I was immediately greeted by a beautiful, thin woman in heels three inches higher than mine.

"Welcome to MTV! You must be Paige, right? The parking attendant told us you were on your way up. Follow me to the waiting room and Michael will be right with you."

Sitting in an oversized red chair, I was a bit nervous. Pulling out my phone, I clicked on my Bible app and scrolled through some Scriptures:

"For I know the plans I have for you, plans for welfare and not for evil, to give you a future and a hope." - Jeremiah 29:11

"Commit your work to the Lord, and your plans will be established." - Proverbs 16:3

"Many are the plans in the mind of a man, but it is the purpose of the Lord that will stand."
- Proverbs 19:21

At ease, I knew I had nothing to worry about. If it was God's plan for me to intern at MTV, it would happen regardless of the interview.

Feeling a tap on my shoulder, I turned around to face a man in his early forties wearing thick-rimmed hipster glasses and striped suspenders. He led me to a massive conference room with floor-to-ceiling windows overlooking the Santa Monica pier and bright blue ocean.

We immediately clicked. He was a swimmer, I was a swimmer. We both did triathlons and ran in races and enjoyed the beach. Once we began talking more about the intern position, he told me there were hundreds of online applicants of which he had decided to interview a small handful. The other interviewees, he told me, were media students from USC and UCLA. He said it was rare for him to hire a Pepperdine-er.

"What? Why?" I asked, confused.

"Well, Pepperdine is known for strong faith, and I don't want a conflict of interest. You seem like a very nice, put-together girl, but are you sure MTV is your style? Do you even watch MTV? Do you watch 'Teen Mom?' Or 'Teen Wolf?' What about 'Ridiculousness?' They produce 'South Park' on the third floor, have you ever even seen that show?"

A bit shaken up, I chose my words carefully: "I am going to be completely honest with you, Michael. I am a Christian. I am a woman of faith and that won't change. I'm not an avid TV watcher. I've seen a few MTV shows, none of which I watch weekly. But, I'm a hard worker, I'd like the position, and I don't believe you will be disappointed if you choose me."

Standing up, he showed me around the office for a good half hour, introducing me to staff members and taking me from floor to floor to check out each of the different channel-headquarters. He sent me off with a gift basket of merchandise, telling me we'd be in touch soon.

Receiving an email from Michael the following day, he told me he'd chosen another candidate for the position but thanked me for my time and told me to keep in touch.

I was bummed.

I hadn't gotten the internship of my dreams. The internship I had longed for... dreamed of... for so long. But I soon began to re-evaluate my so-called 'dreams.'

Why had I wanted to intern at MTV in the first place? Michael had a good point - I wasn't much of a TV watcher and hadn't even watched a full episode of anything on MTV besides my short-lived Hills obsession back in high school. Was MTV really the best place for me to flourish and thrive? Would it allow me to be creative in the ways I envisioned for myself? Would it fill me up? Would my time there help make the world a better place?

I had applied at MTV simply because it was cool. I wanted an internship at MTV just to say I had an internship there.

Living for the approval of others is a dangerous path to tread on, yet I had fallen victim to thinking an internship at the highest ranking television company must be my dream, right? Lots of girls at Pepperdine would have killed for that interview, so obviously I should have wanted it too, correct?

We are wired differently. There is nothing wrong with interning at MTV of course, but it didn't line up with my personal dreams in life.

Not getting the position ended up being the best thing that could have happened to me that year. I immediately started interning at a church, Calvary Chapel - Malibu, and took a job at the Malibu Health Club. Faith and fitness: my two passions.

My words of wisdom? Let's trust God to lead us down the right path. Let's not compromise our dreams, no matter how exciting someone else's may look. Let's own it. Let's live it. We are the bosses of our own life.

Following our hearts, we should do things we don't even look at the clock while doing. We should do what we do best, not based on what we think will make us more appealing to others. If we're authentic, we'll eventually meet a man doing things we really, truly like.

Why attract someone while living a lie? We're too special for that nonsense, beloved.

Chapter 7:
The Big Man Upstairs

"I do not have anything figured out. That's why I call on God to help me through what I can't do on my own." - Justin Bieber

Long ago, there lived a notoriously wealthy man named Baron Fitzgerald. He was one of the richest men in all of England in the early 1800's, and everyone in town knew his name. If he walked into a market, people shook his hand. If he rode down the street in his carriage, people waved. If he popped into the governor's palace, he was treated to a 5-course dinner.

Baron, most notably known for being an avid art collector, didn't let his wealth get to his head. He was a family man. He married the love of his life at a young age and she bore him a son.

Tragically, his wife caught a fever due to the plague and died quickly. Crushed, Baron chose never to remarry. As an only child with deceased parents, Baron decided to devote himself entirely to fathering his son, now a teenager. That is, until Baron's worst fear came true: his son also became ill and passed away.

Meanwhile, Baron's finances steadily increased, and he continued to collect classic art pieces by Picasso, van Gogh, and Monet, acquiring a massive collection rivaling all others in Europe.

In time, Baron also died of old age without any family and few close friends. In his will, he asked for an auction to be held for art connoisseurs to bid for the beloved pieces.

The auction was the talk of the town, and people from all over Europe filed into the city's great hall for the big event. Baron's attorney was in charge of the auction and began to read from the will, which explained how the first piece to be auctioned was a small painting by an unknown artist.

It was the only painting in the collection not painted by a notable artist, and it was a picture of Baron's son, a boy not many in the room had known well. The lawyer opened the floor for bidding, but no one offered a thing.

"Anyone? Anyone at all?"

After a prolonged silence, a poor servant who had taken care of Baron's son raised his hand and bid an offer of less than a pound. With no counter-offers, the painting of Baron's son was sold.

As people started to rub their hands together for the real paintings to get auctioned, the lawyer slammed his gavel and announced the auction was over. Immediately in an uproar, the audience asked what he meant.

"What about the rest of the pieces? The van Goghs? The Picasso's? What do you mean it's over?"

Unfolding the will, the lawyer began to finish reading the remainder of Baron's instructions.

"Whoever bids on the portrait of my son, my beloved boy, the apple of my eye, gets it all. They get every single painting in my collection."

And with that, the auction was indeed over.

God, like Baron, is the beholder of a vast wealth of treasures that go well beyond our thinking. He holds the key to everlasting life in Heaven, with streets of gold and sun shining all day long. There's nothing but joy and laughter and praise.

God is willing to give us incredible treasures if we do one thing: honor His son, Jesus, and metaphorically "buy" his painting.

I've often heard people tell me they refuse to become Christians because they see God as a hypocrite.

"Why would I worship a God who only lets certain people into Heaven? Why do we have to believe in Jesus to get in, why can't He just be accepting?"

That's the point, He is accepting! He wants everyone to be in Heaven with Him, which is why He sent down His son in the first place!

Heaven is a place where Jesus reigns. He'll be the one everyone wants to grab their morning coffee with. So, why should God allow anyone into Heaven who doesn't want to hang out with Heaven's #1 celebrity?

Someone once told me we can measure our treasure by what death can't touch and money can't buy. Baron knew he would be dead. He didn't care about making any money at the auction. All he wanted was for his son's name to be remembered, just like how God see's Jesus. He doesn't care what baggage we bring to the table or how broken we are, He just wants us to honor His son.

Out of all the wealthy people at the auction, the one who walked away with the prize was a poor servant who cared for the boy. Funny, isn't it? We don't need to be anything special to acquire the wealth of Heaven, He'll take anyone who simply says 'yes.'

I find myself getting caught up in trivial things: "Does that boy think I'm cute? Have I gained a couple pounds? Do people find me successful?"

Reading the story of Baron forces me to take a step back. Honoring God's beloved Son is all we need in this life. As long as we accept Jesus and live a life honoring His name, the treasures someday awaiting us are beyond comprehension, far exceeding anything we could ever have in this life.

Many friends of mine get down on themselves about being single. Instead of feeling full from the love of Christ, they feel empty for lack of a man so they do everything they can to find a boy.

And why not? What's the harm in dating?

Before realizing Christ was enough, I felt I had an obligation to find a boyfriend. I liked the idea of feeling protected, thinking a boyfriend would instantly help me feel loved and cared for. I wanted to hear I looked pretty, and I longed to have a boyfriend to text me cute messages. If I had someone, I wouldn't have to be alone and face my problems.

Since then, Jesus has shown me true life, allowing me to bask in His glorious presence and feel His security always. My patterns of serial dating were nothing more than empty snatches at happiness. True love doesn't exist without Him; He alone provides real satisfaction. Even the best boyfriend in the world couldn't outdo the love of Jesus!

Contrary to society's lies, singleness is nothing to scoff at. It's the most beautiful, peaceful, Godly time of our lives. When else can we put all of our time and energy into a relationship with our one true Prince?

To clarify: dating is not wrong. But we can leave the details to the Lord and kiss the idea of 'serial dating' goodbye. We don't need to worry about searching for a future husband; God will provide. Instead of searching for a man, we can give God the pen to write our love stories with no intention of taking it back.

However, being content in Christ is tricky if we rarely spend any time with Him. What boyfriend would like a girlfriend that called him only once a week just to ask for some money for a new purse? Not a single one. God's the same: He'll fulfill our needs and desires, but He wants a real relationship with us first, not just a text once a week asking for something.

I remember the first time I ever felt God speaking to me. My freshman year of college, I was recruited to swim for St. Bonaventure University, a private college located in upstate New York.

My roommate at the time was another swimmer and ironically also named Paige. A few weeks into school, Paige invited me to spend a night at her house in Buffalo. I agreed.

After picking up Mighty Taco, a Buffalo-based food joint locals obsess over, we pulled up to her house, a gorgeous two-story overlooking a quiet pond. Trying to figure out what to do that night, her boyfriend called to tell Paige he had gotten off work early and wanted to meet up.

We met her boyfriend and one of his friends out for wings. Now, just a side-note, people in Buffalo are total wing snobs and have no problem admitting it. Buffalo Wild Wings (a personal favorite of mine!) is basically boycotted - they only go to the authentic, local joints.

Feasting on a double order of medium wings with secret sauce, it was starting to get late - nearing midnight. I figured Paige and I would head back to her house. But out of the blue, her boyfriend had a suggestion: "We should go to Niagara Falls!"

A little taken aback, I couldn't help but blurt out, "Wait, what?! Now?"

"Come on! Live a little!"

Shrugging my shoulders, I was only in college once, right? "Well, um, okay... I'm in!"

Piling into Paige's car, we made the 30 minute drive to Niagara Falls, arriving as the clock struck 1:00 AM. We found a parking space (obviously - no one was there) and climbed out.

I had never been to Niagara Falls. In fact, I had never seen a legitimate waterfall before. Nonchalantly chatting away with Paige and her friends, it was extremely dark and I couldn't see the falls as we walked. I could, however, hear the intense roar of the crashing water, sounding like smoke bellowing out of a train, thick mist coating against my face.

Making our way to the edge, I heard the noise getting louder and the mist getting thicker. It was almost eery, in a way, being there so late without a soul around.

Stepping up to the railing, I took my first glimpse of the falls, and it immediately took my breath away. Standing right next to the waters falling point, I couldn't believe how massive the falls were. The water raced fast as a bullet, charging until it plummeted down the insane drop.

Taking it all in, even though my friends were veterans, we didn't speak a word. Grabbing a stick off the ground, Paige's boyfriend threw it into the water, watching it get swept up and immediately thrown down the falls.

Walking up and down the walkway all alone, we continued to appreciate the scenery, allowing the mist to coat our faces. The few words we did say were drowned out by the booming noise of the crashing water, so we kept our thoughts to ourselves.

I didn't grow up in a sound church and found Christianity boring, frankly, and I didn't become a follower until two years later. I wasn't completely sold on the existence of God. This particular night, however, I couldn't help but be blown away - finding an inkling of a thought that, hey, maybe God was actually there?

Sometime's it takes something massive - switching jobs, a new family dynamic, an illness - to get our attention. That night, the sight of Niagara Falls was massive, both literally and figuratively.

"Is God really there? Did He actually create this enormous, breath-taking, awe-striking waterfall? If so, what more can He do for me? Can He create things in my life too, just like this waterfall?"

Something about the whimsical adventure, the recent lifestyle change, and the fact it was nearing 2 AM ended up being the perfect elixir to spark some Jesus questions.

Driving back to Paige's house, we were all exhausted, for good reason, and I began to doze off in the backseat. Eye's half closed, looking out the window, my mind drifted back to the question of God.

"If He could create something like that, He could probably do anything He wanted, couldn't He?"

Realizing God has infinite power was hard to grasp, but once I was able to accept His presence and His help, my world changed. Knowing the same God who created Niagara Falls, the moon and stars, Mount Everest, and the human brain actually loves us and has a plan for us is life changing. With God as our Father, what do we have to fear? Who can stand in our way?

I now don't struggle with doubting God's existence like I used to. My struggles are different - it's more about wondering if He really has a plan for me.

I'll catch myself asking things like: Am I ever going to find a man like all my girlfriends? Am I ever going to have the perfect wardrobe? Am I ever going to move out of this town? Am I ever going to lose these extra 10 pounds? Am I ever going to feel special?

I need to stop asking 'Am I?' and meditate instead on the great 'I Am.' He spoke the world into existence in a matter of seconds and can speak anything into our lives. Who cares if I'm single my whole life? Who cares if I stay in this little town in Wisconsin? Who cares if I don't live a life of excitement and jetsetting and exploring - what's the big deal? The powerful 'I Am' loves me, what do I have to fear?

He came down to Earth from His Heavenly throne so we could join Him in Heaven forever. While He was enduring the pain on the cross, you and I were on His mind.

When we take our last breath here on Earth, we will take our first breath in either Heaven or Hell. The beautiful thing is, those who believe Jesus died for them won't have to worry about a thing because He covered it all.

But herein lies the problem: lots of young women choose to ignore what Jesus did for them. The other day in the newspaper, I read how the percentage of Christians in the world has dropped and atheism has grown, making atheism the #2 most popular "religious category" people associate with, growing from 16% to 23% in the last seven years.

People are caught up in the fast paced living of wanting things fast, often seeing God as an old-fashioned fun-spoiler.

Look at dating for example, why wait for who God has for us, if anyone at all, when we could download Tinder to line up a date for tomorrow night?

The danger is this: people without a hope in something greater are far more prone to fall for lies: needing a drink or five to cure the pain, a stick thin body to be worthy, or a boyfriend to feel loved. As a former sufferer of an eating disorder, I am the first to attest my Godless life was a broken life.

Our limited days are too fragile to pretend God's not real. Those who open the door to Him will find He's been standing there waiting all along, complete with two hot cocoa's and a roll of calorie-free cookie dough, able to help with anything we need.

As women, we are programmed to please. We love relationships, thriving on helping others feel comfortable and cared for.

Yet, we often forget to love and care for ourselves! I've found, oddly enough, the more I love myself (going for a long walk with my iPod, having a solo coffee date with God, writing in a journal) the easier it is to love my family and friends. Metaphorically speaking, my cup must be full in order to pour into the cups of others.

Taking time for ourselves may sound slightly egotistical, but even Jesus Christ, the son of God, set aside time for Himself. "Jesus would often slip away to the wilderness and pray alone" (Luke 5:16). Taking some solo time allows for a clear heart and mind, leading to less self-depreciation and belittlement.

Alone time fills our cups. Before we know it, we'll be overflowing into everyone else's. They'll be dying to know our secret.

Nothing can satisfy our hunger the way a relationship with Jesus Christ can; He's the water that quenches our thirst, the cupcake that satisfies our sweet tooth, and the light that shines our path. He's the world's best carpenter, fully qualified to shape us well beyond our imaginations.

Esther, a favorite Bible character of mine, was a young commoner living in Persia. Her parents had both passed away, leaving her with her uncle, a Jewish man. After hearing of the saving power of the Lord, she decided to invite Him into her heart for herself.

Meanwhile, the king of the province was on a search for a wife, and the most stunning women in the country were called together to partake in twelve months of beauty treatments to be presented before the king.

Esther was one of the lucky women chosen for the treatments, and the king was immediately smitten by her beauty and grace. Out of all the women who underwent the treatments, the king chose young Esther to be his wife. A grand wedding ceremony shortly followed, and her family was given palace quarters, forever changing their lives.

Through her devotion, Esther was no longer a common woman, but queen of the land. God wasn't finished with her, either, years later using Esther's political standing to save the lives of thousands of Jews.

God took a lowly orphan, put a crown on her head, and used her to save His chosen people. Esther was a nobody, but once she accepted the Lord, He turned her into a sparkling beauty. God's specialty is turning nobodies into somebodies.

The same God who gave Esther a lasting legacy wants a relationship with us, asking us to hand Him our messes. In return, He'll take care of everything! He'll handle our insecurities, our futures, and our relationships. He'll carve us into beautiful masterpieces. He blesses His children above anything they could ask for, giving them all they could ever need: love, peace, patience, guidance, inner-beauty, and everlasting joy.

Whether He leads us down a path to become a queen (like Esther) or a housewife or a missionary or a schoolteacher, God knows where we each belong.

The world's most beautiful women are those who not only know who they are, but whose they are. And you, beloved, are Gods.

Chapter 8:
Where's My Man?

"I wish I could go back and find you sooner. That way, I would love you longer." - Drake

Lately, I've been debating the idea of getting my own place. I graduated from college in California, moved to Guatemala to serve as a missionary for a few months, and have been living with good ol' mom and pops back in Wisconsin. I do love it, but the idea of having my own home sounds appealing.

Long story short, I prayed about it and decided to stay home for a bit longer, seeing as part of me envisions myself venturing off again, but I still toured a couple houses just for fun. One of them was well over $1 million, which I obviously could not afford.

It was straight out of 'Better Homes and Gardens.' It rested on a private beach on Lake

Michigan with a big white gazebo, a flower garden, and a long, winding driveway.

I've become interested in interior design and architecture, and this particular house hit everything on my dream wish list. It was right across the street from a private school I could potentially send my future kids to, it had a beautifully designed outdoor deck, and the landscaping was impeccable.

After spending about an hour roaming the house, I started to feel empty inside. I started to feel discontent with what I had, feeling like I needed:

this house
a husband
3 kids
a white, fluffy labradoodle
a jet-ski, pontoon, and speedboat
a country club membership

...like, pronto. I started thinking about all my friends with husbands and homes and little babies. I started to think about how behind I felt for not having any of them. I started to feel embarrassed, wondering if all this "waiting on God" was really going to pay off.

Feeling down on myself, I read God's word:

"My Father's house has many mansions; if that were not so, would I have told you that I am going there to prepare a place for you?"
- John 14:2

Lusting after a life I don't have is no way to find contentment. Jesus is preparing a mansion for us in His personal Kingdom - a mansion better than even the 'HGTV' Dream Home!

The point of our faith is hope in our eternity in Heaven. The sad part is, hope of eternity is something I rarely ever think about. I think about this Earth and the things I'd like to do and accomplish during my short life here.

Why am I not thinking about spending forever with Jesus in the land of "golden streets" and "emerald walls" and a "sea clear as glass" with "no darkness" and "eternal joy?" I mean, duh?

I don't need a mansion. I don't need a husband. I definitely don't need a jet-ski, speedboat, and pontoon. But I do need Jesus!

We never know what God will bless us with. Maybe someday by the grace of God I'll wake up in that house with a Godly man by my side. Or, maybe I won't. It doesn't matter either way because in 100 years it'll be gone. By then, you and I will be relaxing in our Heavenly mansions playing golf with Moses (hey, you never know)!

In the meantime, let's remember "our God shall supply all our needs according to his riches in glory by Christ Jesus." (Philippians 4:19) Amen, sister!

Yet, contentment is a struggle. I get it. During my time in college, I would hear people voicing their desires for a 'ring by spring,' referring to the longing for an engagement before college graduation. I was surrounded by girls (and guys!) scrambling to figure out their plans. Graduation was swiftly approaching, and the fear of a disappointing future was real.

As a young girl, my dream was to become a princess. Watching Disney princesses sparked fantasies of wearing a flowing gown and sparkling tiara with handsome Prince Charming at my side. I'd clutch his waist as we'd gallop on a big white horse toward lavish picnics overlooking our kingdom. Prince Charming would draw his sword on evil forest villains, protecting me at all costs.

Growing older, I continued to crave a prince. I wanted someone to look into my eyes and tell me everything would be alright. I itched for a warrior to protect me from the insecurities of my awkward teenage years and solidify my worth in the world. I hungered for a relationship so badly, I opened my heart to all the boys portraying any remote interest in me.

The chain-dating didn't lead to Prince Charming. Instead, it led to heartache, grief, and bitterness. Why hadn't I found the man I fantasized about? Would I ever find a prince? Did a man like him even exist?

Even after accepting Jesus, I still wanted a man right away. But, the beauty of our faith is that we already have a Husband waiting for us! Our true Husband awaits us in Heaven. One day we'll meet Jesus as His beloved bride and share a massive wedding feast with Him. Even if we never get married on Earth, we have a wedding awaiting us in eternity with the greatest Husband of all. He loves us so much, He's setting plates at the ballroom tables right now, anxiously awaiting our arrival!

God alone meets our needs. Waiting times are sweet times. Many people glamorize marriage, holding it on a pedestal representing everlasting happiness. Although a Godly partner can certainly sweeten one's life, it will not meet every desire. It is better to remain single than to marry the wrong man!

Once Adam placed Eve's importance higher than God's, both of them fell and sin initially entered the world. Idolizing a husband or wife, even before we meet them, can be disastrous. Without finding total satisfaction in Jesus, marriages are bound to crumble. Expecting an imperfect person to heal our heart is placing far too heavy a burden on them.

A 'ring by spring' can be great, as long as both partners keep their eyes on the Author and Finisher of their faith: Jesus Christ. He's the ultimate bridegroom, fully able to "grant our requests," (Matthew 8:13) "bless us," (Matthew 10:13) and "save us" (John 10:9). Talk about a real Prince Charming!

Instead of daydreaming about make-believe Disney-prototypes of princes, I've found peace in the greatest Prince of all. The "angel of the Lord will stand in the road with his sword drawn protecting us." (Numbers 22:31) He has an "everlasting dominion that will not pass away and a Kingdom that will never be destroyed." (Daniel 7:13-14) Jesus will "reign forever" (Luke 1:31) with the "armies of Heaven behind him, riding on white horses and dressed in fine linen." (Revelation 19)

Our Prince awaits. Meanwhile, we can become His perfect princess.

Over 2,000 years ago, God looked far and wide for a suitable woman to bear His only Son, keeping His eyes peeled for a willing servant. He examined the heart of every woman on Earth, looking for a humble, generous, meek, Holy woman.

Having His choice amongst the most beautiful, rich, talented, elegant women in all eternity, He chose to overlook them all. He was searching for someone different; someone He could use as an empty vessel to pour His mercy into. He finally selected His gem. She was no princess; instead, a young, poor woman engaged to a modest carpenter.

He sent His personal messenger angel, Gabriel, to tell her of the great and marvelous plans He had for her. Gabriel shared how "favored she was in the eyes of the Lord." He explained how her son, Jesus, would be given the highest throne in Heaven with an unending Kingdom.

God knew exactly what He was doing when He chose an average, ordinary woman. There was nothing different about her compared to other women. Nothing, that is, except for her heart.

Because she held onto no idols except the Lord, she was usable.

God chooses simple, shy, and ordinary people to be leaders in His church. He casts a shadow over the proud and offers a furnished throne-room in Heaven to those we'd least expect.

Moses was hesitant to be a tool for God. "Please, Lord, I have never been eloquent... for I am slow of speech and slow of tongue... why would pharaoh listen to me?" (Exodus 6:30) He figured God could find someone better suited for the job, not finding himself worthy of a great calling.

Jeremiah, a renowned prophet, had similar resistance, "Oh, Lord God, I really do not know how to speak well enough for that, for I am too young." (Jeremiah 1:6) He felt his youth disqualified him from being used as an instrument.

The prophet Isaiah understood his unworthy nature. "I am undone, for I am a sinful man with filthy lips, yet I have seen the King" (Isaiah 6:5). Isaiah didn't feel fit to be in Gods presence.

God can most certainly use us, just like He selected Moses, Jeremiah, Isaiah, and Mary.

Are our hearts ready and willing to bow down to His plans? Will we accept His offer to be His warriors like the others before us?

Jesus sees His daughters as "favored" just like He saw Mary. He offers us protection and love no other man can.

Recently, I read a book titled 'Your Beautiful Heart' by Lauren Scruggs, a fashion journalist who has reported from the red carpets of the Milan, Paris, and New York fashion weeks. She had it all: fame, looks, and a future. Until one day, she was stepping out of a small plane and was hit by the propellor, slicing off half of her arm and an eye.

Believe it or not, Christ used her accident to showcase His greatness! She wrote the book after the incident about how she still knows she's beautiful because she's a daughter of Christ.

She now has a prosthetic arm and eye, but she's more beautiful than ever. She met her husband, Jason Kennedy, sharing her story on the set of E! News where he's a reporter. He knew she was the one for him within seconds.

In the foreward of the book, Jason writes:

"Even from across the studio, I noticed her smile. It was one of those smiles that, even on your worst day, would make you feel better. After such a terrible accident, Lauren could have chosen not to smile and to view the world with bitterness and pain. And yet she was smiling. I wanted to get to know the woman behind that smile."

For a long time after the accident, she didn't think anyone could ever find her beautiful. But God had Jason for her, just like He has someone for us, too. No matter how badly we feel about our exterior appearances, we are flawless in the eyes of Jesus.

Speaking of appearances, the Bible doesn't say much about appearances at all! Our society is obsessed with how people look, but the Bible doesn't even mention one detail about how the star character, Jesus, looked.

It says there was "nothing beautiful or majestic about His appearance, nothing to attract us to Him. We turned our back on Him and turned the other way."

But how can we get a visual without any details? Was he tall? Did he have freckles? Or a man-bun?

The only details we are given about appearances of Bible characters are as follows: Esau was hairy, Jacob wasn't. Leah had dull eyes, her sister Rachel didn't. Saul was tall. David was handsome. Eglon was overweight. Zacchaeus was short.

The Bible is jam-packed with heroes and villains. But what story is complete without accurate detail on the characters' looks? What's the fun in that?

The fun in that, beloved, is proving how God can and will use anybody, no matter how tall or short. He doesn't care if we have perfectly shaped eyebrows or have landed under 120 on the scale. He does care, however, if we have a heart desiring His help.

God goes where He's wanted. Those who call upon Him will be made new! The Bible says to "knock, and the door will be opened." Be encouraged by the story of Lauren Kennedy. She is now more beautiful than she's ever been - she's found her worth in Christ, beauty at its finest.

Placing our heart in the hands of God, He will place it in the hands of a man who deserves it. Meanwhile, we can use our time of singleness to go on dates with God and realize just how beautiful we really are. Quiet time with God is never wasted.

A friend once gave me great advice, saying "if we can't stay consistent with God, it'll be even harder for us to stay consistent with a man." He'll write us a love story that will not only fulfill our desires but will serve to encourage those around us. God knows the exact day the right man will walk into our lives because He's pre-ordained everything.

God gives His best to those who wait on Him. We have nothing to fear with Him on our side.

Chapter 9:
What's Mr. Right Thinking?

"Three things I want in a relationship: eyes that won't cry, lips that won't lie, and love that won't die." - Wiz Khalifa

I stumbled upon a rather strange television show titled "Married at First Sight." People signed up to be analyzed by a group of 'love doctors' in order to be matched up with their future spouse. The kicker: their first face-to-face interaction was at the alter. Pretty intense, if you ask me, but hey - who am I to judge?

Reality TV tends to draw a massive bandwidth of followers. Who wouldn't be intrigued? These people were handing their entire future over to a group of so-called 'experts' to choose their SPOUSE, for goodness sakes! For-better-or-for-worse, richer or poorer, grow old together, his-and-hers-bath-sets marriage. Nuts, I tell you. Nuts.

What was running through their minds before walking down the aisle? Would they find their match attractive? Or charming? Or friendly?

Sometime's I wish I could sign up for something like that and take all the work out of dating. I sometimes wonder if there's anyone out there for me. "How will I ever find the right person living in this small town? Is there really someone who'd want to spend the rest of their lives with me, of all people?"

Thankfully, God is just like those love doctors - except more accurate and without the television cameras. He gives us specific desires for a reason: so He can fulfill them. Learning to dance with God, He can allow the right man to step in. Instead of worrying about making ourselves more "appealing" or "cool," we can do what we love, whether that's joining an underwater basketweaving club, a yodelling club, a beatboxing club, or writing a book about relationships (like yours truly). Out of the blue, the right person with similar interests will pop in. That's what God does: He takes joy in surprising those who trust Him.

We don't have to sign up for a reality show to find the right person. We don't need to hire "love doctors." We don't need to message any boys on Facebook. We instead need to get off of Facebook and get our face in THE book (of God)! Spending time with Him is never wasted. The closer we grow with Christ, the more we'll know what to look for in a future spouse.

"But where is God hiding all these great guys? I don't see them anywhere!"

Contrary to popular belief, there are hundreds - even thousands - of single, classy, sexy Christian men looking for someone with more than a pretty face. Christian gal's often find themselves pessimistic thinking strong, manly, rock-solid men are few and far between. But ladies, rest assured: they are out there, and they are worth waiting for.

We will not find anyone perfect, even the boys on the Abercrombie bags or the men in boy bands (sorry again, Nick) have little lifestyle hiccups. But we, as Christ's daughters, are worthy of good men who not only make our heart pound, but stir up our lives for Jesus regardless of small imperfections.

As Christians, we don't need to worry about searching under every rock for someone holding those important qualities above. All we need to do is love God with all our heart, and He'll bring the right man to our door. And who knows, maybe one day Nick Carter's single, Christian cousin will give me a holler? (nudge, nudge)

Once we've handed our future marriages over to Jesus, then and only then will we truly find a knight in shining armor. Meanwhile, we can do our best to become the best version of ourselves, allowing God to prepare our hearts for our future.

"But Paige, how do I know God has someone for me? It's pretty risky to just 'hand things over to Him.' What kinds of things are guys looking for?"

Good point, lovely. Men know what they want. Just last night I asked my 20-year-old brother what he wanted for dinner. "Tilapia, sweet potato, brown rice, and green beans," he texted back within about three seconds. Whether it's regarding dinner, their dream car, where they'd like to live, or their favorite sports team, boys rarely hesitate to explain preferences. This includes, of course, the type of woman they'd like to spend the rest of their lives with.

Women, when asked what they think men look for in a potential Princess Charming, are quick to answer: Thin with the right curves, long flowing hair, the right amount of sex appeal, tan skin year round, thick lashes, polished nails, nine-inch heels... the list is endless and the struggle bus has arrived. Striving to become "worthy," women often over-burden themselves to try to have a perfect exterior in order to fit the bill for what their "dream man" may be looking for. Frankly, it's an exhausting process with no finish line.

I have a man-friend (ahem, not boyfriend) who is God-fearing, attractive, smart, and kind. He's tough yet incredibly gentle. He's currently pursuing his degree in law with a bright future ahead. Trust me when I say he has his pick of women, yet he's taken a step back to allow God to choose his wife for him. Having asked him a few questions, I was able to dig deeper and see what real men look for in a woman. (and no, his phone number is not in one of the questions)

1. What are some attributes you desire in a future wife?

"A lot of Christian men look to Proverbs 31 for some biblical direction on what attributes we should desire in a future wife (a.k.a. suitable helpmate). However, there is one passage that speaks even louder to me found in 1 Peter 3: "Your beauty should not come from outward adornment, such as elaborate hairstyles and the wearing of gold jewelry or fine clothes. Rather, it should be that of your inner self, the unfading beauty of a gentle and quiet spirit, which is of great worth in God's sight." I literally love that passage. I desire to walk alongside a woman who has a gentle and quiet spirit- the kind of beauty that simply does not fade. I imagine that kind of beauty only becomes more radiant with time. What a blessing that is. She HAS to love the Lord more than she loves me. I am human and there will be days where my love simply fails, where I am inconsiderate, where I let her down, where I momentarily forget who I belong to (Christ). If she loves me more than she loves God, she may be in for unnecessary disappointment. The Lord has an unfailing love, meaning it does not disappoint, it isn't inconsiderate, it never lets us down, and it always stays true. If she is rooted and grounded in that Love even on the days where I fail in my love, she will be completely whole and even be able to forgive me for my shortcomings with the Love she herself has received from the Lord Himself."

2. What should a Christian woman be praying for her future husband?

"She should pray he Loves the Lord more than he loves her. She should pray the Lord faithfully continues to grow in him what he needs to be a suitable helpmate for her as she prays the same for herself. She should pray they will be presented to each other at precisely the right moment. She should pray he leads spiritually with all humility. She should pray that he has a sensitive heart. She should pray if children are desired he will help train them "in the way they should go". She should pray he never puts anything before the Lord, not even her."

3. How do you feel Christian men differ from men in the media in regards to finding a spouse?

"As a man, who spent a great deal of time sensitive to the flesh and not sensitive to the spirit, I understand the viewpoint the world uses to find a spouse. While still spiritually immature in this regard my criteria had little to do with what we find in the Bible. It was flesh driven. "How beautiful is she, how curvy is she, will my friends be impressed when they see me with her?" Basically the world tries to convince us we can make love out of lust. You can not. God is love, and therefore the glimpses of true love we get to experience are forged from and through HIM. Ask yourself: Is the work you can do for the Kingdom of God greater with this person than it would be apart? If the answer to that question is yes…. you are on the right track."

4. What would you say to encourage single Christian women?

"Your identity has nothing to do with how anyone else views you. Your identity has nothing to do with how you view yourself at times. Your identity has everything to do with who Christ is and what He has done for you. Christ calls you beloved. He gave His life to you and has been wooing you from before you were born. He showed you He loved you and then waited for you. As you wait for a husband, never forget Christ thought you were worth the wait. "While we were yet in sin, Christ died for us." (Romans 5:8) Before you loved him, He loved you. He shows us what it means to wait patiently. This season of singleness is a gift- as I find myself single as well. Christ is your spiritual main squeeze and is preparing you for your suitable main squeeze. Trust that He knows what He is doing. Trust His Love - That He unbelievably, undeniably, unrelentlessly, unceasingly, unendingly cares for you. Trust His Ability - That He CAN do it. Trust His Sovereignty -

That He WILL do it. Trust His Timing - That at precisely the right moment it will happen."

Needless to say, he is the type of man God can't wait to give us.

Meanwhile, we can try writing a letter (or thirty) to our future special someone. Once our wedding day arrives, we'll have an amazing present to give. What's more romantic than saying "I loved you before I even met you?"

Believe it or not, lots of men (cutoff wearing, football watching, hand-me-another-beer men) write letters, too! Dolls, we may not be the only ones giving a "mailbox" surprise on our wedding day!

A man-friend of mine, just as handsome and charming as the one I interviewed above, shared a little secret with me: He writes letters to his future sweetheart! Believe it or not, he was graciously willing to share a recent snippet, asking me to keep his name anonymous.

"Dear babygirl,

I've been single a couple years now, going on the occasional date but nothing serious. Sometimes I'll accompany my friends out for a few drinks, but the girls I meet out are few and far between. I'm pretty sure I haven't met you yet, I feel like I'll know when we meet. But less about me, more about you.

I promise to care for you with every inch of my being. I promise to protect you, helping you see just how beautiful you are every single day. I promise to compliment you on how you look in the red dress I bought you and how good your blueberry pancakes are and how much better at yoga you are than me. I promise to hold your hand until we are 100 years old, never forgetting how lucky I am to call you mine. I promise to never drop the D-word; we'll be in it for the long haul, and I'll never speak of regret. I promise to sing along with the radio, as awful as my voice is, making you laugh. I promise to kiss you goodnight, to make you my favorite chili because you will not be vegan☺, and to go to those cheesy romance movies with you. I promise I'll respect your mom and learn from your father and call him sir.

I pray you have a heart for Jesus, becoming my better half and pointing to the Gospel whenever I fall. I pray you're patient with me, because I'm far from perfect. I pray you're sweet and kind. And most importantly, I pray you make a mean steak and potato dinner.

I love you already. I'm making mistakes along the way, but I entrust our future to Christ. Love you baby girl. See you sooner than later, promise.

Love, your man"

What gal doesn't want a husband like that? He's the type of man who will pamper his future wife. And he's the exact type of man God plans to surprise us with.

I personally cannot wait to be with the one God is preparing for me, but I'm also thankful for the men I already do have in my life: my brother and my daddy. Witnessing my brother James's life has given me an inside scoop on how boys work, think, and play. I've learned the NBA is actually quite entertaining if you legitimately sit down and watch. I've learned (20 year old) boys really can eat everything in the entire kitchen and still have room for a #5 sub from Jimmy Johns. And I've learned boys don't have things as easy as us girls seem to think they do.

I may be biased, but my brother is one of the most handsome boys I know. He's 6'3" with blonde hair and a swimmers body (he is a college swimmer, after all), and he's got a lot going for him. He has a great coaching job, a family who adores him, and friends he sees on the reg. Yet, even James struggles with the occasional ping of insecurity and self-doubt.

The male ego is much more fragile than women know. James is no different than any other man in the entire universe. All men suffer at some point in their lives with their worth, talents, life plans, body image, and reputation. Not one of us, guys or gals, is perfect - not a single one - and we know that first hand. We live in our bodies, so we see every single mistake we make, from sleeping past our alarm to cursing under our breath to BAD breath!

The Bible gives a clear vision for Godly women. Women are to be gentle-hearted, servant-like, helpful, encouraging, and loving. But what about the men? The Bible is filled with male characters who serve God with courage (David), submission (Job), stubbornness (Jonah), faith (Noah), vigor (Paul), and peace (Jesus). It's almost overwhelming how many men the Bible contain, and they all seem to have different attributes. Some are total opposites of each other!

All men are created differently, but men are still men. Our leaders. Our warriors. Our princes.

Every (burly) man I've talked to in the last year seems to have seen the movie 'American Sniper.' I refuse because anything too intense or scary is not for me. If there's a scary scene while I'm at the theater, I usually conveniently need to fill up my popcorn in the lobby.

Anyway, from what I've heard, one of the scenes from the movie involves the main character as a little boy listening to his father's advice.

"There's three types of people in this world: sheep, wolves, and sheepdogs. Become a sheepdog."

His father was explaining the importance of leading the innocent and helpless to safety, away from the wolves. I believe the Bible expects all men of God to be sheepdogs, so that's exactly what us gals should look for.

While the "wolves" of this world try to justify how men should use women as objects, live promiscuous lives, watch porn, and cheat on their significant other, true men of God (sheepdogs) steer the sheep (a.k.a. younger men) away from the lies of the wolves and into safety. A true man of God knows how precious a Godly life is. It's up to them to teach other men how to become sheepdogs, not wolves.

A true man of God also knows his true worth. Lots of boys struggle with their appearance. I so often ponder how tough the world is for girls, with magazines of photoshopped celebrities in bikinis and skeletons walking down the runways of Milan. But the struggle is just as real - if not more real - for men. Men are told from a young age they've got to grow up big and strong, just like their superhero action figures.

Basically all the guys I've dated asked me if I thought he was muscular enough or needed to lose fat or workout more or take more pre-workout protein (or even get on steroids!). There's always a pound of fat to lose or muscle to gain. I challenge all women of Christ to wait for a man who knows his worth is in God, not how many pounds he can bench or packs on his abs. God created all men to serve Him and love Him, yet many men (and women!) get so easily caught up in appearance and forget their one true purpose on Earth is serving Christ.

Women who love Jesus are looking for men who love Jesus. Men set the spiritual thermostat of a family; if the man doesn't pray before dinner time, why would he expect his wife and kids to follow God? Would a man rather see his daughter reading "50 Shades of Grey," or the Bible? Men were born to be leaders. Godly men should strive to set the thermostat through the roof.

The legendary Johnny Cash once said, "Being a Christian isn't for sissies. It takes a real man to live for God – a lot more man than to live for the devil." We're God's daughters, so we don't need to spend our precious time chasing someone God doesn't want us to have. A real man worships God, not sex or money or violence or power. The mate God will send us will bless us, not burden us. We have nothing to fear when our God is near. The only thing we have to fear is allowing our lusts to overcome our rightful thinking, because God won't bless a relationship He's not involved in.

We are women of God, looking for more than someone who can pay a tab at restaurants. We're looking, and waiting, for men with Jesus in their eyes.

Paige Nicole Weslaski

Chapter 10:
Preparing For the Big 'I Do'

> "Love one person, take care of them until you die. You know, raise kids. Have a good life. Be a good friend. And try to be completely who you are. And figure out what you personally love. And go after it with everything you've got no matter how much it takes."
> -Angelina Jolie

Half of me can't wait to be married. I can't wait to wake up next to someone, to make coffee for someone, and to go on lifelong dates with someone. But, to be honest, half of me is absolutely terrified to be married. What if he gets bored of me? What if we realize we're not meant to be?

God tells us "not to worry about tomorrow" and to instead worry about being the best version of ourselves we can be today. The better we are today, the better wife we'll be down the road.

I began to wonder what us women can practice, and it hit me: gentleness. Godly men look for gentle woman with a peaceful spirit and a loving heart.

In today's society, women are taught to go after what they desire, be it men, money, or power. Women on television tend to be loud, provocative, and crude. Growing up, I had very few role models in the media with concrete morals.

In God's Word, women are advised to be respectful, to learn "quietly and submissively, refraining from talking over men." Women should practice modesty and decency, remembering there's nothing more attractive to a man than a woman with quiet confidence.

A gentle, modest, loving character gives light to the face that cannot be duplicated even by the best cosmetics. Outer beauty is worthless if a woman is obnoxious or cold. Grooming and decoration starts at the heart and works its way outwards.

Practicing composure through turmoil is the key to unlocking a gentle spirit. When

Abraham's servant was looking for a wife for his master, he approached a well and found a "very beautiful woman old enough to be married." After asking her for a drink, she answered elegantly and kindly: "Yes, my lord. Have a drink, and I'll even draw water for your camels, too," and she ran back and forth between the well serving the man. He instantly knew she was the right woman because she went above and beyond to serve him.

My pastor told me he instantly felt attracted to his wife because of her gentle, servant-minded attitude. The first time he met her, she was at LAX airport asking her father for help with her passport. Humbly asking her father for help showed her humble mindset and respect for authority.

During their first month of dating, she invited him over to her house for dinner. Although he wanted to help in the kitchen, she sat him down at the table and stated "sit down and let me serve you." She enjoyed the idea of serving her man, making him feel comfortable and special. He knew her gentle attitude was no act; it was ingrained in her character. He knew right away she was the one he'd been waiting for.

Just as important as our character - us ladies should commit to maintainting purity.

Now, this is a personal subject for me because before accepting Christ, I was not practicing purity. I did not understand the sacredness of waiting for one person.

I remember back in 2010 how the Jonas Brother's used to wear purity rings - signifying they would stay sexually pure prior to marriage. I remember thinking it was a bit much.

"With the fame, money, and looks, who were they trying to kid? And, what was the big deal about being with someone prior to marriage, anyways? How old-fashioned."

Since then, the tables have turned. I am the first to admit I've screwed up in that arena, but having found Christ, I understand and fully agree with the purity ideology. Nick Jonas on the other hand, who took off his purity ring long ago, has started singing about 'Jealousy' and 'Chains.' Come on now, Nick!

People found it funny the band wanted to wait - including me - but honestly, what's so funny about choosing to be with one person? I used to find that crazy; how could people wait so long? It was only sex, right? What was the big dealio?

The dealio is with each person we go to bed with, we give away a piece of our heart. I, as well as many of you, know that personally.

Lust is the counterfeit of love. What's the difference between the two? True love can wait, lust can't. True love is others-focused, lust is greedy. True love is fully content, while lust is never satisfied. Waiting for marriage creates a tremendous amount of trust between a couple, lust creates insecurity and obsessiveness.

This is the part where I put on my big-sister baseball cap, so be forewarned. The world wants us to believe sex is breezy and no big deal, and I once fell victim to that fabrication. If I was dating someone and we "loved" each other, it was all good, right? Every other girl I knew was sleeping with their boyfriend, so what was stopping me?

I've met young women who've grown up in Christian families, many of whom wear purity rings. A few months ago, one of those girls told me she was waiting on sex for marriage, but also - to kiss! I couldn't believe it. I literally could not tell you how many boys I've kissed in my life. I would need a few more sets of hands just to count.

Now that I've seen the damage it's done to my heart and thought-process, I wish I could trade places with that girl. She's drop-dead gorgeous and could easily kiss seventeen boys today if she chose, yet she made a promise to herself to commit fully to her future hubby. Now that's love.

So, having done just about everything the Bible warns not to do, I'd say I'm certified to share my opinion: to wait. Breaking our purity is not worth it. Any man who won't wait for us is not worth it.

Look at it this way: a true knight in shining armour should do everything in his power to keep us pure, right? If a boy gives an ultimatum, sex or the door, we can cheerfully skip our way out, delete his number, and move on.

Be encouraged, ladies, because great marriages do still exist, free of insecurity and jealousy. The question is, will ours be one of them? Rapper B.O.B., as rocky as some of his lyrics are, nailed it with these lines:

"With no directions just tryna get some
Tryna chase skirts, living in the summer sun
This is how I lost more than I had ever won
And honestly I <u>ended up with none</u>."

Let's not give our hearts or bodies away until the time is right, beloved. If we've already tripped up, do not fear. Christ is more than willing to forgive, cleanse, and restore. We should respect ourselves before we wreck ourselves, we'll be thankful later.

Through the saving power of Christ - no matter what we've done, we can still wear white, both literally and metaphorically, on our wedding day.

It's important to make these decisions prior to jumping into a relationship because people in love lose their minds.

Now, that is not necessarily a bad thing. I've loved lots of things: peanut butter dipped pretzels, french manicures, watching the sunset on Zuma beach… And because of that love, I sometimes do outlandish things. I'll make a detour at Whole Foods just to munch on the pretzels, I'll pay an arm and a leg for my French mani-pedi, and I'll drive 15 minutes just to watch a 60-second sunset. I'm a lady in love, and I don't overthink the consequences. I want what I want.

Being in love is a game-changer. I've had a handful of boyfriends and I've said those three delicate words to three or four of them. If I meant them is a far different story. In the moment, I figured I did, but looking in hindsight, I'm shifty.

People shot by Cupid's arrow tend to believe things not necessarily true in order to protect the temporary ecstasy of love. I've seen it time and time again.

A girl will accept a date from a guy well-known for being no good, figuring it's only "one night and no big deal." One night turns into two, two turns into ten, and before she knows it, she's head over heels for the type of man she never wanted to get involved with in the first place.

Before I became a Christian, I hung out with all types of guys because I wanted to feel worthy and accepted. Today, it's more of a rarity to see me on a real date-date aside from the occasional coffee shop run-in with a guy friend, but that doesn't mean I'm not tempted to date the wrong type of guy.

I also bring up this topic because, on a personal note, five couples I know filed for divorce in the last twelve months. Five. Couples with 20+ years under their belt and young kids in need of a stable home.

Every Saturday all over the world, weddings are held bringing two single people together as one. Those singles repeat a set of vows before tying the knot. Vows like: "I'll love you from this day forward, for better, for worse, for richer, for poorer, in sickness and health, until death do us part."

The sad part is, lots of people who say those vows do not mean them. In the weeks leading up to the wedding and at the actual event they may think they mean them. They may believe it with every inch of their being. But, if they haven't put in any personal preparation, the vows will fall flat.

I like to compete in triathlons. I love the swimming, biking, and running. I love the cheering of the crowd, the adrenaline in my veins, and the feeling of zipping past competitors. But, no matter how excited or pumped I get for a specific triathlon, I won't cross the finish line without putting in the training. I could promise others and truly believe in my heart I'll win, but if I'm not doing any training, it won't happen.

Marriage vows are like triathlons. It takes preparation or else they're bound to fall short.

How can someone prepare for their wedding vows? Not by studying up on the tips in Cosmo or learning how to make Creme Brulee or buying expensive lingerie. Those things will come. Proper preparation for holding true to wedding vows throughout ones entire life starts by preparing to commit.

Preparing to commit to someone, as a single woman, can sound a bit outlandish, but it'll make marriage that much sweeter and easier. Commitment to a future spouse means not flirting with everyone in town, not saying yes to every date offered, and not giving away our phone number as if it were candy.

"Well then, how am I supposed to meet someone, Paige?"

Simple. The right man, the one God has predestined you to marry, will fight for your attention out of respect. He'll notice and honor your values of self-worth and will treat you with dignity and class because you'll deal with nothing less.

If you make it a priority to commit now, it's very likely you'll marry someone who themselves prepared to commit, too. Your lives will be moving in such similar directions that anyone who's not going in that direction will be a conflict with your values. You'll find yourself uninterested in frogs.

All of life is interconnected. What we did yesterday affects today. What we do today affects tomorrow. How we handle ourselves will affect who we ultimately end up with. We should 'become the person that the person we're looking for is looking for,' meaning we need to get serious about today's decisions. We should become whole and healthy before diving into a toxic relationship to fill a hole in our hearts.

If we find ourselves starting to fall for someone, we need to take a step back and look at their past decisions. What kind of a person are they? Do they have a solid job? Do they have a strong faith? Do they honor their family? Do they surround themselves with positive role models?

And we should ask ourselves: if we were a boy, would we be best friends with them? If not, the relationship is probably not for us.

Let's stand strong. Just today I had to stand strong and block a couple guys from social media because I don't want to get caught up in daydreaming about Mr. Wrong. We can't let the craziness of attention blind us. We need to prepare ourselves now so we end up right where we belong. We can't let ourselves be treated without respect.

The other morning, I read a great article titled "Why Chivalry is Dead, From a Man's Perspective" by John Picciuto (Elite Daily). Picciuto makes the argument guys aren't 'manning up' to treat women with the respect they deserve. Some men are no longer treating to dinners, opening car doors, or being the men their fathers and grandfathers used to be. Here's a snippet:

"Dating is done. Seriously, who goes on dates anymore? It's all about hooking up, getting a number, grabbing a drink and getting down. I think I'm the only single guy I know that actually takes a girl out to a restaurant on a first date."

He has a good point. Many men aren't owning up to the fact they are, well, men. The article takes an interesting turn, however, and the writer begins to explain how, although men need to step it up, women are just as guilty of hurting our society's dating expectations. We're becoming complacent, allowing men to "get away with adhering to the bare minimum." He explains:

"Us men no longer have to put in the effort of flowers, chocolates, dates, etc., and if we do, we come off as stage-five clingers. Women need to wise up and start asking for the things they deserve, the things which used to be automatic and expected of men, like holding a door, pulling out a chair, and paying for dinners. Until then, men are going to get away with putting in the bare minimum. It's pretty obvious women own the cards, and when they start acting like it, they'll finally start getting dinner from places that don't deliver."

My oh my, he has a point! John wasn't afraid to speak the truth: us women have convinced ourselves we're satisfied with being treated sub-par. Consequently, men realize they no longer need to fight for us. Nice dinners, opening doors, and treating a woman with respect is no longer necessary.

With the massive feminist movement the last century, women have grown more and more independent, which is wonderful. The right to vote, (general) equal pay, and more opportunity has led to wonderful things for the common woman. But, does that mean we no longer need to accept help from a man?

The way I look at it, today's man wants a woman of strength and confidence, who enjoys taking care of herself and others. Todays man does not, however, want a woman who demands independence, undermines chivalry, and takes the "male" role in a relationship.

Men are taught from a young age to work hard for what they want. Why would a man feel proud to be with a woman he didn't have to work for? Men want women they have rolled out the red carpet for, whether that means cooking for her, taking her to nice places, or telling her she looks beautiful.

I'm not saying men need to spend thousands of dollars on their future wife, but they do need to put in time and effort. Otherwise, have they really fought for her? Would they really feel proud to be with someone without having to lift a finger?

It's our duty, princesses, to raise the standards, to not settle for men who don't treat us well, and to expect chivalry. It's for our best and their best. The gender roles will not be confused, we'll feel like a princess, and he'll know he's fought for something worthwhile.

According to a study in the UK, 90% of men consider themselves gentlemen. If we expect our future man to be a gentleman, he will be one. He knows how, it's in his genes. We shouldn't laugh at him for opening the door, demand a split check, or try to text him first to set up a date. Let's let him do the work. In all honesty, he'll appreciate it.

This time of temporary singleness is a special time to prepare our hearts and minds for our future man. We need to become the person the person we're looking for is looking for: women of gentle spirits, women of purity, and women of integrity.

Chapter 11:
Will We Get Our Fairytale?

"Initially you think, a Victoria's Secret model! Holy cow! Then that goes away and all you're left with is the person."
-Adam Levine, Maroon 5

Let's be honest with ourselves. Who has never once wanted to be a Victoria's Secret model? They literally look like angels (hence their nickname) and seem to be the most care-free women in the world. They've got style and they've got almost every man drooling over them. Who wouldn't want a piece of that pie?

Last year, I was out to lunch with a friend of mine at a restaurant in Malibu called Plate. It's one of my favorite places of all-time, and I've ran into a small handful of celebrities eating there; Reggie Miller, Adam Sandler, and Brandon Jenner in particular.

It's a quiet, locals-only joint tucked away on Pacific Coast Highway overlooking the ocean.

The tourists tend to choose Duke's a mile down the beach, which in my opinion is a bit overrated.

My friend had graduated the year prior and was living in Colorado but came back for a weekend visit. I picked her up from her hotel and we headed over to Plate for brunch on a Saturday morning. We sat down at a table near the front window and ordered our meal. She ordered banana pancakes and I ordered an omelet with fruit and toast, both of us asking for their famous green juice and coffee.

We had both become Christians the year prior, so we chatted about what God had been doing in our lives. I explained how worried I was about where I'd end up after graduation, and she started telling me about how her life in Colorado was quiet and she'd found a nice church.

Facing the window, we watched as people carried their groceries out of a boutique grocery store called PC Greens and carried their bags to their 6-figure cars. We watched as men in chef hats carried gluten-free pizza pies out of D'Amores Pizza for delivery. And we watched as a gorgeous woman stepped out of a two-door Ferrari arm-in-arm with a muscular, bald man in a suit jacket.

The woman was wearing black and white striped pants, a black tank top, a fedora cap, and big, white glasses that formed complete circles. Her blonde hair fell to her shoulders, and her slim body made it quite obvious she had done lots and lots of squats in her lifetime.

I knew I recognized her, but I couldn't put my finger on who it was. Immediately, my friend pinched my arm.

"Paige!" she whispered. "That's Rosie from Victoria's Secret!"

The celebrity couple sat at the table next to us as our food was set at our table. As I reached for my fork, I heard my conscious speaking. Setting down my fork, I asked my friend if she minded if we prayed before we ate.

We bowed our heads, thanked God for the meal, and said Amen. As we looked up, we noticed Rosie and her boyfriend looking at us. It was hard for them not to, to be honest, as their table was only about two feet away.

Not a whole lot else happened. My friend and I continued to talk about God. Rosie ordered a veggie wrap on whole wheat. We finished our plates and signed our bill. Rosie asked for a green juice. We left the restaurant. And that was that.

Rosie is the type of woman every girl wants to be. But without placing her trust in Christ, even Rosie doesn't hold the key to eternal life. Us women get so caught up in wanting to look and act a certain way. Many of us would do anything to have the life Rosie has. But that's just the point - this life here on Earth is so teeny tiny compared to Heaven.

Leaving the restaurant, I felt a sense of overwhelming peace. Rosie was the woman I always wanted to emulate, and it wasn't a surprise God placed her within an arm's reach away from me. Sure, she was gorgeous. Sure, she had a hot boyfriend. Sure, she owned the cutest pair of pants I had ever seen. But that day I realized I was no different than her. God calls all of us His children, no matter how we look or what we say or where we work or who we date.

I left a part of myself at Plate that day: the part that compared myself to others. We are children of the living God, used by Him and adored by Him and uplifted by Him. No matter how many fans Rosie has on this Earth, there's only going to be one real celebrity in Heaven, and that's Jesus. Sitting next to Rosie allowed me to see that, although incredibly beautiful, she's only human.

I've always been a fan of Victoria's Secret. I like their clothes, especially the Pink brand. But I've found something even better: the 'victORIOUS secret' that Jesus loves us and wants to spend eternity with us forever, no matter who we are.

Jesus isn't worried about how the world see's us. Having spent so many hours agonizing over my appearance or my weight or my popularity, thinking I needed to impress boys in order to feel beautiful, Jesus couldn't care less about my appearance or resume.

Take a peek at the men He chose to be His followers. Jesus walked up to a group of four fisherman and asked them if they'd like to become fishers of men instead of fishers of... fish.

All four were immediately mesmerized by Jesus They dropped their nets and joined His entourage for the next three years without so much as saying goodbye to their family and friends.

Let's say Jesus didn't come 2,000 years ago. What if He had decided to come down today instead? Let's pretend He still wanted an entourage of twelve people to join Him on a three-year mission around the world. What type of people do you think He'd choose?

If I could choose anyone in the world to be in my entourage, I'd be so selective it wouldn't even be funny. I'd choose the smartest, prettiest, most famous people I could think of. A brain surgeon, the investors from Shark Tank, the President... I'd want smart, capable, driven people around me.

Fishermen were not high on the totem pole in Jesus's time. They were low, and just about anyone could join a fishing crew without real training.

That apparently didn't bother Jesus, because He didn't choose just one, but four. They traveled with Him, ate breakfast with Him, laughed with Him, and cried with Him.

Jesus didn't choose the men by coincidence. He didn't randomly walk up and choose the first men He saw. He sought them out, choosing them to be His sidekicks. They were men who probably swore like sailors, went days without showering, and laughed at inappropriate jokes. They were blue-collar men.

So who would Jesus pick if He came down today instead? I'd assume He'd select normal, every-day people. Maybe a plumber, maybe a taxi driver, maybe a factory worker, maybe a waitress; he'd choose people with willing hearts and nothing to lose.

Jesus finds people without much to offer (by the world's standards) and uses them in mighty ways. People with a heart to learn and a humble mind. Jesus is not the exclusive, judgemental man we so-often make Him out to be. Jesus is 'one of the guys' and wants to hang out with someone as mediocre as you and me. The Bible explains how God plays no favorites, He just loves those who love Him.

Someone like the gorgeous Rosie could have almost any man she wanted. We may not have that luxury, but we do know we're wanted by God. All of us women who believe in Christ are therefore more beautiful than anyone on Earth because we hold the purity of Jesus in our hearts. Hip-hip-hooray!

We may not have a line of boys trying to date us, but true men of God will see us not for our exterior but our interior. Instead of holding our heads down, stressing over every imperfection on our own bodies, God calls us to hold our heads up high to see every perfection of Him in Heaven. It sure takes the pressure off ourselves when we rest our identity in the God of the entire world.

Earlier I mentioned how the night I accepted Christ I broke up with my boyfriend, a man whom I saw as perfect in every way. The only problem? He wasn't as in love with Christ as he was with me. He didn't help me pursue my faith the way I knew I needed to be led.

But what if he would have been a man of God? What if he had been a Bible-thumping, church-attending, Christ-focused follower of the Lord?

In all honesty, I would have done the same exact thing. That's how badly I needed a time of singleness to focus on God.

A time of singleness for any young lady is a time of centering; of figuring out who we are and who God is. At that point in my life, I was struggling in many areas, particularly my body image. My freshman year of college in New York, I gained the freshman 15. Transferring to Pepperdine in Los Angeles the following year, I wanted to lose weight to ready myself for the new school.

I lost weight. Too much weight. I went overboard, losing about 50 pounds. I went into my new school weighing 110 pounds, which for a 5'9" gal with muscle from swimming was not okay. Not okay at all.

After a few weeks on the swim team, I was pulled aside by the athletics nutritionist and asked if I could meet in her office. She measured my body fat and was frightened at what she saw. She immediately sent me to the on-campus hospital to see a doctor. I was placed on the Pepperdine eating disorder treatment team, seeing counselors, doctors, and nutritionists weekly.

After meeting with the doctor a few times, I still didn't gain weight. I kept losing. Until one appointment scared me straight:

"Paige, as your doctor I need to be straight with you. If you come to your next appointment having lost even one more pound, you will be forced to pack up your bags and leave Pepperdine. Do you understand? You're a liability. Do you realize how low your blood pressure is? Your heart could stop beating any second. You'll need to check into a facility immediately if you don't turn this around."

I was taken off the swim team on an "injury" leave and didn't have a lot of friends at the school. I was feeling lost and didn't know where to turn. My parents flew out from Wisconsin on weekends to help me gain weight. A few breakfast buffets later, I slowly put on some pounds.

I soon began to get more involved on campus. I joined a sorority, the campus newspaper, and the campus television station, starting to feel more at home.

Then, I met my boyfriend at a party.

I was drunk, he was drunk, we kissed, and I woke up to a message from him on Facebook asking to hang out.

My birthday was coming up that weekend, and I had invited a group of girls to go to Club Avalon in Hollywood with me. I rented a limo, and all the girls wore black dresses while I wore white. I mentioned the plans to him, and once we walked into the club, he was there with his posse.

The rest was history. We started hanging out often. I stayed with him and his family a couple times at their home, and he met my family during their trips to LA. It seemed perfect.

The only problem was, I was still harboring an eating disorder. I had gained the weight back, but my eating habits were far from healthy. I'd starve myself all day, living on apples and vegetables, later binging on anything and everything.

It was a dark life. I'd be so proud of myself for restraining from food, and then I'd feel a weight of guilt after eating anything.

I of course hid this from him, as well as from everyone else, acting as if I was free as a bird. But in reality, I was still a slave to an eating disorder.

The night I became a Christian, I knew I needed to change - I just didn't know how. I knew I needed help escaping the chains of my detrimental eating habits, but I couldn't do it myself. I had tried everything: writing down everything I ate, eating specific diets, and speaking with counselors, but nothing could heal my problem.

That is, until I met Christ. I knew He could help me like He helped people 2,000 years ago.

One day, Jesus was touched by a woman in a large crowd who struggled with menstrual bleeding for twelve long years. She spent all her money on doctors and remedies to heal the problem, but it only made things worse. It wasn't until she reached out to Jesus that she was healed for good.

Likewise, I needed Jesus to heal my problem. I needed him to heal my anorexia. I needed him to heal my binge eating. I needed him to tell me everything was going to be alright, that even though I couldn't escape on my own, He held the keys to let me out of the jail cell I myself had locked.

It didn't happen overnight. I struggled with my eating for a period after accepting Him, but it grew easier and easier. The deeper I grew to Him, the less obsessed I was about my body image.

I wanted to be the best-looking version of myself, so I did everything in my power to stay as thin as I could. What started out as a harmless diet turned into a life of slavery to reach a never-ending perfection.

Singleness is our time to reach out to Jesus and let Him heal those deep-set pains in our hearts. It's a time to walk away from the world of living for others in order to live for God. It's a time to make our faith a personal faith, to allow Christ to be the man we're ultimately living for.

I wanted to be thin to impress my friends and my boyfriend. But once I stopped trying to impress others and instead tried to impress God, I began to feel more self-confident than ever before. He was all I truly needed, and dates with Him were more fun than dates with any prior man. I no longer needed to put on an act. Jesus knew the real me better than I knew myself. With Him, I could be the genuine me.

The most beautiful part of all? I know the man God has for me will be impressed by my faith, not my appearance. I don't have to worry about impressing every man in town, God will take care of all the details to link me with Mr. Right. (not Mr. 'Right Now')

Bob Goff, a professor at Pepperdine and writer of the bestseller "Love Does," was impressed by his wife without her having to do a single thing. He saw her from a distance and was immediately mesmerized by her, placing a peanut butter and jelly sandwich on her car every day until she accepted a date from him. A little strange, but hey, it worked!

Don't stress about finding the right man. Before you know it, you just might find a peanut butter jelly sandwich with your name on it from a man who respects your faith.

And trust me when I say there are Godly men out there looking for Godly women. I recently had a boy from my high school message my blog saying the following:

"I am not the most devout Christian, I tend to find myself worshipping more internally than externally, but deep down I want a woman of faith who stays faithful through all the hard times."

"In the end, if a woman can't stay faithful to Christ in the worst of times, how can I expect her to stay faithful to me? If a woman can't humble herself to Christ when she needs help, how can I expect her to seek my help when she needs it?"

"I've learned the only real way to meet the one you're meant for is purely through patience. Trying to force something that isn't, or be someone you aren't, only leads to more headache and heartache."

There are countless men of God out there looking for women of faith and integrity. A man is out there waiting for a heart like yours -

a heart of inner confidence and outward submission.

Real men are looking for women with a sincere faith. Like my old high school friend said: "How can a man take a woman seriously if she doesn't even give Christ the time of day?" Real men date women who love Jesus. That boy is the type of guy with a PB&J in hand waiting for the right girl's car to place it on.

As God's princesses, we deserve a man who treats us well and cherishes us as much as we cherish Christ. The boy from my high school is looking for someone he can care for, but who can also care for him.

God's got someone out there He knows will fit perfectly into our lives; someone who will roll out the "red carpet" for us, whether it's a dinner at the Ritz, picnic in the park, cookie decorating in his kitchen, paint n' sip at a cafe, a hike in the woods, or a dancing club in the city!

When I studied abroad in college, I spent a month in Germany and a month in Italy. My friends and I traveled all throughout Europe; we rented mopeds in Florence, ate and drank our way through Tuscany's finest cafes and vineyards, enjoyed operas, symphonies, ballets, and plays, toured castles and churches and monuments, relaxed in Italian spas, and ate far too much schnitzel and too many croissants.

We rode a gondola in Venice, took a bike tour through Barcelona, made our own pasta in Italy, got lost in the Florence leather mart, jumped into the Cinque Terre ocean, and drank lots of different types of German beer in the pubs. Needless to say, it was a grand time, a time to try new things and test the waters on living life to the fullest. There's a time and a place to try everything (to an extent), and it's called Europe.

I was a bit of a hopeless romantic, and I of course daydreamed about meeting a 6'5" Ralph Lauren model during my trip. I had watched the "Lizzie McGuire Movie" before I left (I know we've all seen it five times so no need for judgement) and was thinking how exciting it would be to meet an Italian pop star and travel on the back on his Vespa.

I did not meet a popstar. I did, however, meet an incredibly handsome man named Marc. Living in Germany's premier college-town, Heidelberg, the town was brimming with pubs and hangouts. One particular Saturday night, my friend Stephanie and I ventured into a pub.

There was a DJ and flashing lights, but absolutely no dancing. We were a bit confused, as it was late, a prime dancing hour, and we there was not a single foot tap in the room. We later found out German clubs are much different than those in America. Dancing is a no-no.

We were approached by two men, one who was blonde and the other was tall, dark, and handsome Marc. Marc and I hit it off right away; he spoke pristine English and worked as an advertising executive. Stephanie and her blonde man fizzled quickly; his English was sub-par and they didn't click. Marc and I exchanged numbers, and he asked me to accompany him to dinner the following night. I said yes.

Our Pepperdine abroad class was living in a chateau overlooking the city, and with Stephanie by my side I got dressed up and awaited his arrival. Hearing a honk outside the house, I looked through the window and down the three flights of stairs to the main road.

There was Marc, dressed in a full suit and tie standing with a bouquet of fresh red roses holding open the door to his brand new BMW convertible.

I felt like a princess walking down the stairs to her carriage.

Handing the roses to me as I eased into the passenger seat, I knew it would be a great night.

We arrived at the Italian restaurant a bit early, so we went for a little stroll over the Neckar bridge, talking nonstop as if we'd known each other for years. Walking into the restaurant, he poked his head into the kitchen to say "buon pomeriggio" ("hello!" in Italian) to the chef, of which he'd known forever.

Marc ordered dinner for both of us in perfect Italian, and we talked the night away, ending the night with espresso shots and a brownie biscotti at a gelato parlor down the bridge.

Marc and I went out a few more times, one of which we drove 283 Kilometers per hour on the autobahn with the top down, but that's another story for another time. (sorry, mom)

Marc and I no longer keep in touch; the last I talked with him he had moved to Switzerland to work in bank marketing. But I learned a lot from dating Marc - I don't need to settle for a man who doesn't remind me of a real Prince Charming. There is nothing wrong with holding a high standard when it comes to whom we date. Jesus Christ sees us as princesses inside and out. Too often in my life I've settled for someone who didn't treat me with much respect, which in turn led to me disrespecting myself. I've been burnt in relationships because I've played with fire, dating someone I knew wouldn't treat me like the "beautifully, wonderfully made" woman I am.

We can't underestimate our worth. We end up with the exact love we think we deserve. You and I deserve a strong man, just like men deserve strong women who respect themselves.

When we go on a date, we have a few things to ask ourselves:

Is this the type of man that will respect me forever? Do they help me shine? Will they help me achieve my dreams? Or do I have to hide who I really am?

We are worthy of a prince. If we respect ourselves, we'll attract someone who respects us, too.

Now, I'm not recommending we all fly to Europe to find our future man. This story took place before I became a Christian, and I probably wouldn't have gone out with him if I was a believer, seeing as I most likely wouldn't have been at the pub in the first place.

We don't need men who drive brand-spankin'-new BMW's or drop buckets of money on us at fancy Italian restaurants that aren't Olive Garden. We don't even need men who speak fluent Italian (although, it was quite charming)!

But we do need men who treat us with respect and love. We need men who have a heart for Christ, which Marc unfortunately lacked.

How do we find a man who loves both us and God? By dancing with Jesus. Once He's taught us the steps, the right man will step in to lead us on this giant dance floor we call life. God won't choose just any man, but a man who knows the steps of the dance perfectly, too.

Instead of falling for the wrong man (no matter how nice his car may be!), we can pray for God to keep blinders on our eyes like a racehorse. Instead of looking to the left and right at all the men in math class, the office, or the gym, we can keep our eyes on Jesus. He'll bring the right man in without us turning our heads once.

The famous Holocaust survivor Corrie ten Boom once said "prayer should be our steering wheel, not our spare tire." Regularly praying for a Godly mate can allow for God to ready our man before we even meet him.

God wants our future marriage to be a blessing to us and the world, not a burden. We can stand tall as single women knowing our God is taking care of our futures. The larger we make God in our lives, the smaller our problems will seem. Singleness will look less like a time of loneliness and more like an opportunity for joy!

God is a God of surprises. He promises to give us the desires of our hearts.

Meanwhile, we can spend our free time fearless in our pursuit of what sets our soul on fire. Serving God with no apologies, we can choose a life of G.O.D. (greatness over darkness)

Satan knows our names but calls us by our sin, whereas Jesus knows about our sin but calls us by our names. Instead of listening to Satan's lies to look or act a certain way to find a guy, God knows that couldn't be further from the truth. Jesus blots out our past and calls us to a glorious future with a good-hearted man.

God alone can give us the life we are destined to have. Casting all our worries on Him, we can live our lives knowing He's paving the path of our days.

He's got our love contracts all written up, darling. Really, He does.

The real question is: will we trust Him?

Made in the USA
Middletown, DE
12 April 2021